BUILDING CUSTOMER LOYALTY
from the Inside Out

BUILDING CUSTOMER LOYALTY

from the Inside Out

DEBRA J. SCHMIDT

Loyalty Leader® Publishing
Milwaukee, Wisconsin

Published by:
Loyalty Leader® Publishing, a division of Loyalty Leader® Inc.
P.O. Box 170954
Milwaukee, WI 53217-8086, USA
Tel: (414) 964-3872
Email: info@loyaltyleader.com
Web: www.loyaltyleader.com

ISBN: 9780970712745

Library of Congress Cataloging Number: 2008940391

Printed in the United States.

*This book is dedicated to four of the people
I love most in this world:
Larry, Dave, Adam and Emily.*

Thank you for giving me so many reasons to smile.

PRAISE FOR
BUILDING CUSTOMER LOYALTY
FROM THE INSIDE OUT

Debra Schmidt continues to inspire and challenge our thoughts on what it means to be a customer-focused organization. A wonderful reference guide for every organization interested in continual improvement and business success.

—Robert S. Crookston, CHMM
Vice President
Microbac Laboratories, Inc.

Building Customer Loyalty from the Inside Out *is the best book I've read that offers true-to-life, instantly applicable solutions to everyone who reads it. It is a "must-read" for anyone who has internal or external customers and wants to build successful relationships at all levels of the business.*

—Ann Daane
VP HR North America
Case New Holland

Deb brings a wonderful combination of down-to-earth basics and advanced customer strategy together in a clear, understandable way. She provides great advice and real usable techniques to help make your customers love you! A "must-read" for any company or salesperson who wants to fortify customers as well as build new business!

—Kent Jones
Senior Vice President / Client Results Strategist
3D Exhibits

The staff and clients of EWH have found Deb Schmidt's customer service seminars and books enlightening and inspirational. If you own a business, Deb Schmidt can guide you on developing an exceptional customer service program that will benefit your company internally and externally. We are loyal followers of Deb's newsletters and books!

—Edward W. Hastreiter
President
EWH Small Business Accounting S.C.

Building Customer Loyalty from the Inside Out *has provided our team with guidelines and examples to help us in developing positive relationships with both internal and external clients.*

—Deni D. Naumann
President
Copesan Services, Inc.

The insights in this book are practical, implementable, and fun! While pointing the way to business success, Deb engages employees throughout all organizations to develop more Loyalty Leaders.

—Paula Busby Latta
CustomerCare, VP
Rexnord Industries, LLC

One thing that I really like about this book is that it is so easy to read. It's the type of book that you can pick up and read for a few minutes here and there and always easily get back "into" the material. We frequently use it as a training tool.

—Kim Kahl
Training Coordinator
State Bank of Cross Plains

TABLE OF CONTENTS

CHAPTER 5:
COMMUNICATING WITH CUSTOMERS 165

ACKNOWLEDGMENTS

I am indebted to the many clients of Loyalty Leader®, Inc., who, over the past twelve years, have entrusted their training and consulting projects to me. Through their examples, they have taught me a great deal about what it takes to run a business based on integrity.

In particular, I want to thank Linda Schaefer and Deanna Tillisch of Northwestern Mutual, who believed in me from the start and have not only directed numerous clients my way, but also shared valuable advice and feedback. I would also like to thank the many managers throughout Northwestern Mutual who have given me the honor of presenting hundreds of training seminars for their employees.

My thanks go to the thousands of readers of my online newsletter, many of whom have been subscribers for years. Their ideas and suggestions have provided a rich source of material for my books and training programs. I also want to thank Kira Henschel and Ken Brosky, who both helped me to organize years of articles into a readable manuscript with their publishing knowledge and editing skills.

I'm grateful to my sister, Barbara Bartlein, who inspired me and gave me the courage to launch my own business. It is without a doubt the best career decision I have ever made and I couldn't have done it without her.

I thank my mother for teaching me the true meaning of loyalty and setting an example for me by becoming an entrepreneur in an age when women just didn't do such things.

Special thanks to my brothers, Bob and Rich Bartlein, for sharing savvy business advice and rescuing my computers.

Finally, my love and gratitude go to the two men in my life who have stuck by me every step of the way: my husband, Larry, whose endless patience and marketing ideas have helped me to get through the tough times and grow my business; and my son, Dave, whose wisdom, love, empathy and kindness have made me a better person.

PREFACE

Organizations cannot survive unless they can keep their customers. No matter what your job title, building customer loyalty is your responsibility. It is earned by building positive relationships one customer and one co-worker at a time.

Building Customer Loyalty from the Inside Out will provide you with loads of examples to teach you how to build positive relationships with your customers and co-workers. It is a collection of articles, tips and stories I have been sharing through my seminars, keynote presentations, media interviews, and online newsletters for more than twelve years.

Loyalty-focused organizations consistently outperform their competition. There is no sense acquiring new customers if you are only replacing those customers who have left. In addition to bringing in new business, it's important to turn your existing customers into *loyal* customers. These customers will become cheerleaders who will purchase more products or services—and refer new customers.

As you are reading this book, keep in mind two of the most important aspects of building customer loyalty:

1. It is essential to deliver exceptional service within your organization first.
2. Exceptional customer service starts with a smile!

This book is meant to be used actively. Get together with your team and use these ideas to stimulate discussions on how you can improve service in your department or organization. When you take ownership of service, you will increase your professional credibility and play an active role in the success of your business.

Debra J. Schmidt,
Loyalty Leader®
Milwaukee, Wisconsin

CHAPTER 1

THE FOUNDATIONS OF CUSTOMER LOYALTY

No enterprise can exist for itself alone. It ministers to some great need, it performs some great service, not for itself, but for others; or failing therein, it ceases to be profitable and ceases to exist.

— Calvin Coolidge

LOYALTY STARTS AT THE TOP

Today's businesses are losing customers and employees in record numbers. Customer loyalty and retention is on the decline, but many companies are treating the symptoms instead of the causes. Set your goals to create loyal customers. But keep in mind that customer loyalty starts with the internal customers—employees and co-workers; it's a top-down initiative. It must start with the CEO or business owner. In order to build loyalty, you need to find ways to surprise and delight your employees and customers alike, and exceed their expectations.

Consider the following:

◆   If you're losing employees, you're losing customers. On average, American companies lose half of their employees every four years and half of their customers every five years. This suggests that employee attrition may have a significant impact on customer loyalty.

◆   Employee attitudes are significantly affected by the way they are treated by upper management. One of the most important aspects of improving customer retention is a total commitment to loyalty by the CEO or business owner. This commitment must be demonstrated daily, at all levels of the organization, for the employees to clearly observe.

◆   Customer loyalty is the responsibility of everyone within an organization. In order to create a loyalty-focused culture, customer service training needs to start at the top.

◆   CEOs, business owners and senior management also need to recognize that their employees are their primary customers. Employees expect and deserve the same caring service that is given to external customers.

◆   Customer loyalty is earned by consistently exceeding customer and employee expectations with outstanding service. This level of service can only be achieved when managers are held accountable for their internal customer service skills: in other words, how they deal with their employees and co-workers.

To earn loyal customers and employees, focus on building long-term relationships with each one on an individual basis. Take time to listen to them. Greet them warmly when they call, and use their name at least three times in every conversation. Thank your customers and employees frequently, and find ways to show them how much they are valued. When you focus on building loyalty, both employee and customer retention increase. The end result is a boost in your profits!

PROFILE OF A LOYALTY LEADER

I'm always encouraging people to become loyalty leaders in their organizations. But just what does it mean to be a loyalty leader? It's a commitment to a way of doing business that sets you apart from the crowd. This commitment also extends outside of the workplace and carries over into your community. Here are ten characteristics of loyalty leaders:

1. Sincerely enjoy working with customers
2. Respond very quickly to customer requests
3. Dress and act professionally
4. Anticipate customers' needs and actively look for creative ways to assist them
5. Are honest and trustworthy
6. Follow through on commitments
7. Maintain positive attitudes even under stress
8. Communicate clearly
9. Are patient, careful listeners
10. Actively participate in community outreach

Becoming a loyalty leader is a choice that you make. But it's a choice that can reap rewards, not only for your customers, but also for you personally. This choice will help you to shape your career. Managers are more likely to promote employees who clearly enjoy their jobs and enhance the company image. They don't reward employees who sap the team's energy through negativism and complaining.

It's a well-known fact that negative people can damage employee morale and customer relationships. Loyalty-focused employees create positive energy by focusing on ways to make everyone's day more productive and pleasant. In order to be a loyalty leader, it's necessary to view customers as the reason for your job.

SERVICE AT THE SERVICE STATION

I've been doing business with the same service station for years. The owners are excellent mechanics but their customer service skills have left a lot to be desired. They're both shy and that shyness has frequently been perceived as apathy or even coldness by their customers.

That's why I was taken by surprise when I recently did business with them. My car has been showing signs of age and I had been making lots of trips to my service station. This time, my car had to be there for three whole days. Something quite unexpected was happening. Each time I stopped in to check on their progress, one of the owners came out to greet me with a smile. He chatted about the car and wished me a nice day. He called me no less than five times to give me updates on the parts he had ordered.

Now this was unprecedented behavior by this guy so I was baffled, yet delighted. He said, "Just what is it you do for a living?"

I explained that I'm a professional speaker and trainer who helps companies build customer and employee loyalty.

"Why do you ask?" I said.

He said, "Well, I hope you don't mind. But while I was working on your car, I found one of your audiotapes and I listened to the whole thing. I also noticed that your license plates say LOYALTY. I figured you must be pretty serious about this customer service stuff so I've been trying to do some of the things you talk about on your tape."

I laughed and told him that I watch service very carefully.

He said, "Yeah. I was afraid of that, so I told the other guys to be nice to you when you come in, too."

Let's just hope he sticks to his new method of delivering service. He'll be pleasantly surprised when he discovers how many of his other customers will notice the difference.

GREAT SERVICE IS LINKED TO STRONG LEADERSHIP

There's a famous story about a group of visitors to Disney. They were walking in the Magic Kingdom when they saw a gray-haired man walk out of his way to pick up a piece of litter. One person in the group approached the man and asked, "How many custodians are there here?"

The man replied, "45,000."

The guest was surprised at so many.

The next day, the group attended a "Traditions" meeting and the same gray-haired man was there. His name was Michael Eisner, Chairman and CEO of Disney.

There is a strong link between leadership and great customer service. In over twelve years of delivering customer service training, I've observed that companies with effective leaders are more likely to have employees who deliver great customer service. Great leaders don't just talk about customer service; they demonstrate what it looks like for their employees.

Leaders need to have a vision of what they want to achieve. Few employees will support a customer service initiative that is not clearly defined. They need to understand why they are being asked to do something. The vision needs to be communicated. Let everyone share in it. Let employees see what's in it for them if they follow you.

Great leaders delegate and empower.

That doesn't mean that great leaders simply dump on their employees. They create structure, allocate responsibility, provide support, and offer training and resources. They empower their people to make decisions. This is part of what makes people feel significant.

Great leaders always respect their people.

They treat their employees as their primary customers. Successful business leaders are masters at keeping their people informed. How are we doing? What are we doing? What new things are happening? Newsletters and other internal communication tools should be used to keep employees up to date and informed on the big picture. Key performance indicators are set and explained clearly to employees. Targets are set and success is celebrated. This is how leaders create a sense of community.

Great leaders keep the energy going.

They demonstrate their passion for the company, their vision and customer service through their actions. They have the strength and the energy to work against the odds to achieve their vision. They create a buzz in their organization that keeps the team excited about providing great service.

Research by the Strategic Planning Institute found that those businesses that gave good service grew twice as fast as those with poor service. Great service starts at the top of the organization and needs to be frequently reinforced through training and leading by example.

WHY DO CUSTOMER SERVICE INITIATIVES FAIL?

I have heard it repeatedly from employees in a variety of industries when their company launches a new customer service initiative: "Here we go again. They've tried these programs before, each one with a new name, but they always fizzle out. Why should I get excited about this one?"

Most CEOs and managers begin with honorable intentions for developing a customer service program. They identify the problems and set achievable goals. They invest company resources by hiring an outside consultant or trainer to help them carry out their customer service mission.

Why, then, do so many of these initiatives fail to change the quality of customer service within their organizations? Most likely they are lacking the foundation to support a service culture.

Here are seven key areas necessary for an organization to create and sustain a successful customer service initiative:

1. Start at the top.

The CEO and top management must exhibit a clearly visible commitment to service. This means that there is 100 percent buy-in and support of the service principles by everyone in a leadership role. Managers need to prove to their employees that they believe in quality service by treating their employees with respect, open communication, fairness and integrity.

2. Invest in training.

Telling employees to be friendly is not customer service training. Employees learn solid customer service skills through frequent, interactive training programs. Many companies make the mistake of viewing training as an expense rather than an investment. Training is not a one-time deal. Basic service principles must be continually reinforced. For a customer service initiative to succeed, training must take place throughout the year and be offered in a variety of different formats to keep employees engaged. Training makes employees feel valued. It shows that senior management is investing in their skill development and future.

3. Invite employees to take ownership of service.

For employees to take ownership, they need to understand the "what's in for me" factor. Employees need proof that taking ownership and delivering excellent service will increase the likelihood of promotions, raises and job stability. They need to be able to visualize the big picture and understand how their role in the company affects the bottom line. They also need to be empowered with skills and resources to do what's best for their customers.

4. Reward and recognize employees.

In too many companies, the only time employees receive attention is when things go wrong. One of the primary reasons that employees develop apathy toward customers is because no one recognizes or rewards their good work. Employees need proof that their contributions are being noticed and appreciated. A word of well-deserved praise from a supervisor goes a long way toward developing a positive attitude toward others. A company can follow many successful employee recognition models, but most important are the day-to-day, personal "thank you's" a boss delivers to his or her employees.

5. Develop and enforce accountabilities.

Employees who fail to deliver acceptable service must be held accountable, no matter what position they hold. This is the flip side of reward and recognition. Clearly defined standards let employees know how they will be measured on service delivery. They need to understand when and how they will be evaluated. They also need to be aware of possible consequences, such as little or no raise, or even termination.

6. Build a team spirit.

Involve everyone in setting service goals and identifying ongoing ways to improve service. Train employees to be trainers and mentors to their co-workers. Provide ways for employees to reward and recognize their co-workers for great service. For example, Starbucks employees give each other "MUG" awards for **M**oves of **U**ncommon **G**reatness.

Build the customer service theme into every departmental and company meeting. Communicate customer service principles daily through newsletters, Intranet, meetings and other resources.

7. Celebrate successes.

Post testimonials from customers, print service success stories in the company newsletter, unexpectedly reward an employee for going the extra mile for a customer. Take the whole team to lunch or bring treats when a customer has complimented even one employee for a job well done.

Customer service initiatives can be exciting for employees when companies make a total commitment to developing a service culture. A strong foundation must be in place to support the program before it is launched. However, even the strongest initiatives can fail unless they are infused with fresh training, ongoing communications and creative recognition programs.

BUILDING A
CUSTOMER SERVICE CULTURE

Create a service-oriented culture.

All employees must realize that they work for the customer, and their job is to ensure the ultimate satisfaction of all customers (internal as well as external customers). Every other task is of secondary importance.

Have a service vision.

The vision must involve all employees and be clearly communicated in a consistent manner. Management can develop the vision, but the staff must make it a reality. They need to believe in it and live it.

Write down service policies.

To benefit both your customers and employees, put your service policies in writing. There will be fewer mistakes or misunderstandings. Be sure that employees have the authority to make exceptions when necessary. Remember, policies are guidelines and must remain flexible.

Train your employees.

Train, train and then retrain your employees. Give them on-the-job training, off-the-job training, tapes, books, seminars, workshops and anything else that will help them do their jobs better.

Set clear standards of performance.

Let everyone know exactly what they must do to provide superior customer service. Make these standards as measurable as possible so you can reward great service. When employees achieve these performance levels, customer retention and loyalty will naturally follow.

JOB SHADOWING CAN ELIMINATE SILOS

Groundhog Day was just around the corner, but one year, the groundhog wasn't the only one looking for his shadow. Northwestern Mutual had given new meaning to the word "shadow," with its innovative job shadowing initiative. The company's fast-paced policyowner services department has ten divisions, operating in different locations.

Employees in all of the divisions made a commitment to spend time with one another to share their insights, talents and skills through job shadowing.

Regardless of location or job title, those employees focused on gaining a better understanding of what other teams are responsible for and the challenges they face.

The results? Northwestern Mutual's policyowner services employees are eliminating the "silo" effect.

In any organization, it's easy for artificial boundaries to form between departments and work teams. These boundaries can occur due to physical separation, duplication of processes, lack of trust, management style differences and rapid change. When employees view their departments as separate entities rather than seeing themselves as a part of one company-wide team, it is often referred to as working in "silos." The silo mentality usually results in poor communications and lack of collaboration, making everyone's job more challenging.

Implement a job-shadowing program in your organization. Spend time with employees in other departments. Observe them for a few hours to gain a better perspective and appreciation of what they do.

Ask questions such as:

- ◆ "What's the greatest challenge about your job?"
- ◆ "What do you love about your job?"
- ◆ "What is most helpful to you when dealing with employees in other departments?"
- ◆ "What makes your job more difficult when dealing with other departments?"

Job shadowing will give you an opportunity to learn about how others do their jobs. You'll be able to put faces with the names. A job-shadowing program goes a long way toward building a spirit of collaboration, where employees focus on working together as one united team. This increases idea sharing and support, leveraging the talents and skills of everyone.

YOUR CUSTOMERS ARE YOUR JOB SECURITY

We hear a great deal about layoffs and downsizing today. Some can't be prevented in today's economy. However, other businesses are laying off workers because their customers are going to the competition. Today, clients and customers want much better quality than before. They expect top-notch service or they'll take their business to your competitors. Not your problem? Think again!

Your job security depends on how valuable you are to your customers. The better you serve them, the better you protect your career. If you take your job for granted, you take your customers for granted, and that's a risky way to run a business.

Expect your employer to expect more from you. The marketplace is demanding far more these days from the organization itself. The more you allow your service to go soft, the greater the odds you could end up in some downsizing statistics.

Or, the organization might simply decide to outsource your work. More than likely, you're actually in competition with external providers who offer the same service, whether you realize it or not. In the final analysis, customers are your only source of job security.

WHY SHOULD I CARE ABOUT CUSTOMER LOYALTY?

"I'm not the CEO. I'm not even a manager. So what if customer loyalty boosts the company's profits. I'll never see the money. Why should I care if the customers are loyal?"

Good question, and one I sometimes hear from employees, particularly those who are not in management positions. So what's in it for you to go the extra mile and build customer loyalty? Lots! What do Land's End, Northwestern Mutual, Starbucks, Ritz-Carlton, Federal Express, Disney, Nordstrom, Delta Dental and Stew Leonard's Farm Fresh Foods all have in common?

They are all loyalty-focused companies—and they're all thriving. Loyalty-focused companies outperform their competitors. Loyal customers are more pleasant, purchase more products, refer new customers and are more forgiving when problems occur. This helps to make your company more financially stable. Here's what that means for you:

Job stability

Nearly every time we pick up a newspaper, we read about another company laying off thousands of employees. Certainly there are many factors that cause businesses to fail, but strong customer loyalty can help a business stay afloat even during economic downturns.

Better benefit packages

When a business loses customers, it loses revenue. Period. When it loses revenue, the first thing to go is employees, and next come benefits. A loyalty-focused company like Northwestern Mutual is going strong and still offers terrific benefit packages for its employees.

Career advancement opportunities

A stable company usually offers you the opportunity to climb the ladder and advance your career without leaving. There are more training opportunities available for you to develop new skills and learn about different facets of the business.

No matter how large or small a company is, when it is loyalty-focused, it is generally recognized as a quality place to work. The number one question asked (in an envious tone) of new employees in the companies I listed above is, "Wow! How were you able to get a job there?"

Customer loyalty is the responsibility of everyone within your organization. It is earned by building positive relationships, one customer at a time, by employees just like you.

Take the Customer Loyalty Self-Assessment at the end of Chapter 2 to measure how you're doing on building customer loyalty.

WANTED: FRIENDLY EMPLOYEES

The sign on the door of a local ice cream shop read:

"Wanted: Friendly Employees!"

A dynamic company that advertises great customer service must be staffed by employees who are anxious to provide customer care. Many managers and business owners believe that everybody knows how to provide quality service. Their motto is: "If they don't know, we can teach them."

It is very difficult to motivate negative employees. It's impossible to force someone to have a positive attitude. Negative employees will tend to complain, gossip and sneer no matter how elaborate the training resources are in a company. In order to create a culture of customer service excellence, a company needs to build a team of trainable employees who are easy to motivate.

Here are some tips for hiring the "right" employees:

- ◆ Select only people who are naturally friendly, helpful and people-oriented.

- ◆ Hire people based on attitude first, skills second. Skills can be taught. Attitude is a choice.

- ◆ Hire people who are not embarrassed to provide great service.

- ◆ If a job candidate can't smile during the interview, he or she won't smile at your customers.

- ◆ Communicate to prospective employees that great customer service delivery will be a primary measurement on their performance evaluations.

- ◆ Ask candidates to define customer service excellence during their interviews.

- ◆ Ask your best employees to recommend friends they can be "proud of" for job vacancies.
- ◆ Don't be in a hurry to fill a position with a warm body. Take your time and wait for the right employee. Ask open-ended questions such as:
  - "What's the nicest thing you've ever done for a customer?"
  - "What would your former co-workers tell me if I asked them to describe you?"
  - "What do you think is the most important part of your job?"

If you want employees who will put the customers first, you need to put customer service first during the selection process. Keep in mind that great customer service begins inside the company with the way employees treat their co-workers.

IGNITE A SPIRIT OF SERVICE:
CELEBRATE "CUSTOMER SERVICE WEEK"

Each year, thousands of businesses around the world celebrate "Customer Service Week." It's an international event devoted to recognizing the importance of customer service and honoring the employees responsible for taking care of customers. Start your planning early in order to achieve maximum participation by employees and generate publicity for your organization.

National Customer Service Week is always the first full week of October. Started by the International Customer Service Association in 1988, it has become a national event as proclaimed by the U.S. Congress. According to the ICSA, the purpose of National Customer Service Week is "to create a positive message that lasts all year long and to provide a productive opportunity to generate an even stronger commitment to customer service excellence."

Celebrating Customer Service Week is a wonderful way to show your customers how much they are valued. It is also the perfect time to recognize and reward employees for a job well done by reinforcing the important roles they play in building customer loyalty.

Organize a Customer Service Week celebration in your company in order to maximize these benefits:

♦ Boost morale, motivation and teamwork by rewarding front-line reps.

♦ Raise awareness that customers are the reason employees are at work. Customers are not an interruption of their work.

♦ Generate goodwill by thanking employees in every department for their contributions to the customer service chain.

♦ Thank your customers and remind them of your commitment to customer care.

Event-Planning Tips:

♦ Plan, plan and plan! Lots of advanced planning will ensure that you cover all the bases. A well-coordinated event, with attention to detail, will have the greatest impact.

♦ Encourage members of the planning committee to create activities that are enjoyable for the employees. Make it fun!

♦ Make sure celebration activities don't interfere with customer service.

♦ Create a buzz! Let employees and customers know what's planned and why. Anticipation is half the fun!

♦ Generate publicity. Send news releases to local media announcing your company's plans for Customer Service Week. Invite reporters to attend related events.

♦ Select a theme. You can have one theme for the week or a different theme for each day. The theme will help you select decorations, food, activities and costumes.

♦ Schedule customer service training classes for employees at all levels of the organization to refresh everyone's skills on the principles of building customer loyalty.

♦ Create Loyalty Leader®, Extra Mile or Positive Attitude Awards. They can be presented to employees who have been selected by their co-workers for delivering exceptional customer service. Gift certificates make great prizes.

More tips to help you celebrate Customer Service Week:

♦ Spread the word about National Customer Service Week throughout your organization. Announce your celebration plans to your customers and employees through email, newsletters, posters and even voice mail messages.

♦ Give each employee a small desk mirror to remind him or her to smile when talking to customers.

♦ Once you've developed a customer-focused theme, make it visible throughout the company. Challenge each department to come up with theme-related decorations.

♦ Here are some theme ideas:

- *Smile! Your Attitude is Showing*

- *Customers First*

- *We Care*

- *Customers Forever*

- *Spotlight on Service*
- *Going the Extra Mile*
- *We're All Loyalty Leaders®*

HOW TO CELEBRATE
CUSTOMER SERVICE WEEK

◆ Kick off the week with a motivational speaker to ignite a spirit of enthusiasm and contagious positive attitudes throughout your organization.

◆ Create a schedule of events for the week and post it throughout the company.

◆ Invite a group of your best customers for lunch to meet your customer service reps in person.

◆ Decorate your building with posters, banners, balloons and flowers to create a festive atmosphere.

◆ Give away free candy bars or cookies to customers who come in.

◆ Enclose candy kisses or another type of non-perishable treat with every order you ship during that week.

◆ Send a hand-written thank you note to every customer who orders a product or does business with your company. Have the cards signed by employees throughout the company, even those who only deal with internal customers. Be sure to have them include their title after their signature.

◆ Surprise your employees with bonuses, gift certificates, a day off with pay and other unexpected awards to recognize their commitment to customer service.

◆ Schedule a daily theme or celebration to keep the enthusiasm strong. For example:

- Monday - Kick-off breakfast with a guest speaker.
- Tuesday - Pizza party with a funny movie or skits.
- Wednesday - Stress-buster session with games, fitness tips and team-building activities.
- Thursday - Hollywood day. Everyone dresses as their favorite celebrity.
- Friday - Trick or Treat. Each department serves up a special treat. Employees receive a treat plate or bag and make the rounds to collect the goodies and meet their fellow workers.

Whether you work for a small or large company, you can celebrate Customer Service Week with a one-day event or a whole week of activities. Don't miss the opportunity to ignite enthusiasm for customer care.

SCORECARD FOR BUSINESS
DO YOU WORK FOR A LOYALTY-FOCUSED COMPANY?

♦ Do you work for a loyalty-focused company?

♦ How does the company for which you work measure up when it comes to building customer loyalty?

♦ Is it a place where people want to do business?

♦ Does it easily attract new customers? Do existing customers stick around?

It is a well-known fact that loyalty-focused companies outperform their competitors. Loyalty-focused companies attract and retain great employees. They also have greater customer retention. This translates into job stability, career opportunities and the pride of working for a company that has a reputation for excellence.

Customer service is not the sole responsibility of your customer service department or call center. Customers perceive the company as a whole. They don't make allowances based on a person's title or department. "Oh, he's in accounting, not customer service, so it's okay if he doesn't treat his customers well."

♦ Company-wide service means that every single employee in the organization takes complete ownership of the quality of service they provide.

♦ In order to promote a service-minded culture, companies need to provide customer service training to all employees on a regular basis.

◆   Employees in every department must be held accountable for consistently delivering exceptional customer service to co-workers and external customers alike.

◆   Priority must be placed on the quality of customer interactions during employee performance evaluations.

Go through the following ***Scorecard for Business.*** Give your company 5 points for every "True" answer.

1.   Our company has clearly defined customer standards and they are frequently communicated to employees.
     True or False

2.   Our employees understand that co-workers are their primary customers and that we are all part of a customer service chain.
     True or False

3.   The top managers in our company are required to participate in customer service training.
     True or False

4.   Employees in every department are held accountable for the same quality of customer service that is expected of front-line employees.
     True or False

5.   Our employees are allowed to bend the rules whenever possible in order to meet the needs of our customers.
     True or False

6.   Our employees can recommend a competitor when our company cannot provide the service or product that a customer has requested.
     True or False

7. On performance reviews, employees are rewarded for their excellent customer service skills.
   True or False

8. Employees in our organization feel valued and appreciated.
   True or False

9. Employees with positive attitudes are far more likely to be recognized and promoted.
   True or False

10. Rude or unpleasant employees are terminated after disciplinary measures fail to change their negative behavior toward customers and co-workers.
    True or False

11. Employees are given frequent opportunities to grow professionally and personally through training programs offered in our organization.
    True or False

SCORECARD RESULTS

If your company scored:

45-55 Points—Congratulations, you work for a loyalty-focused company.

25-40 Points—Your company is on its way to being loyalty-focused, but there is significant opportunity for improvement.

0-25 Points—Your company may need to assess its service standards, offer additional training and review customer service accountabilities at all levels of the organization.

CHAPTER 2

DEFINING YOUR CUSTOMERS

There is only one boss: the customer. And he can fire everybody in the company from the chairman on down, simply by spending his money somewhere else.
—Sam Walton

HOW DO YOUR CUSTOMERS BEHAVE?

Have you ever left a store vowing never to return? If you answered, "yes," did you leave because of the way you were treated? Most customers stop doing business with a company because one employee treated them poorly.

Have you ever met a salesperson you did not like? If you answered, "yes," did you buy from that salesperson? Most customers have met a salesperson they didn't like and chose not to buy from that salesperson unless it was a product or service they could not get anywhere else.

Customers and sales are lost every day because of a lack of understanding of the customer's behavioral style. People tend to conduct business with people they like. But style differences often create barriers that can prevent you from building positive relationships with your customers.

My husband and I have very different behavioral styles. When I decide to buy a car, I wait until I can afford a brand-new model. I select the style and color first and I only test-drive the vehicle once. I need to be excited about the vehicle. If I like the way it drives and I think I'll look good in it, the decision is all but made. Once I've responded on an emotional level, it's unlikely that I'll shop around. I prefer working with a friendly, outgoing salesperson who likes to chat. Finally, if the car's in my price range and has a decent safety record, I'll probably make the purchase.

My husband only buys used cars that get great mileage. He reviews *Consumer Reports* to check out safety reports and equipment ratings. He will shop for months and test-drive several vehicles before he makes a purchase. He is turned off by pushy salespeople and would rather be left alone when he's shopping.

Because your customers have different behavioral styles, they are going to like different things. Some customers want:

- ♦ you to get to the point fast and not waste their time.
- ♦ you to schmooze and chat with them for a long time.
- ♦ to buy products with cutting-edge technology.
- ♦ considerable time to think before making their buying decision.
- ♦ risk-free products with a proven track record.
- ♦ to buy based on an emotional response such as excitement.
- ♦ to feel like you're their best friend.
- ♦ reassurance and a feeling of security.

Research conducted by Target Training International, Ltd. has proven that:

♦ People tend to buy from employees who have behavioral styles similar to their own.

♦ Salespeople are more likely to sell to customers who have a behavioral style similar to their own.

♦ Employees who are aware of their own behavioral style and learn to "blend" with their customer's style are able to increase sales and customer satisfaction.

We all have certain behaviors that make us unique. Learn your own behavioral style to help you understand how other people perceive you. There are behavioral style analysis tools that have been around for many years to help you analyze your style. These tools are used extensively by businesses in sales training workshops and they're very accurate. The style analysis assessment tool that I prefer uses a system called DISC® .

According to the DISC® system, developed by Target Training International, Ltd., you can determine your customers' behavioral styles by looking at the characteristics of each of the four styles:

1. *High D* individuals are fast-paced, assertive and strategic thinkers. Their motto is "I want it done now and I want it done right." Other styles perceive them as being too demanding and impatient. Your "high D" customers make buying decisions based on status, cutting edge technology and bottom-line results.

2. *High I* individuals are relationship-oriented. They are outgoing, love to chat and may even give you a hug when they greet you. They're optimistic, enthusiastic and adapt quickly to change. Other styles perceive them as poor listeners and unreliable because they don't pay attention to

details. Your "high I" customers make buying decisions based on emotion, personal image and testimonials.

3.   ***High S***   individuals are soft-spoken and good listeners. They are organized, dependable and loyal. Others perceive them as weak because they will say "yes" when they mean "no." These folks do not like to make waves. Your "high S" customers make buying decisions based on trust, stability, reliability and guarantees.

4.   ***High C***   individuals are analytical and detail-oriented, priding themselves on accuracy. They tend to be quiet and hold their emotions inside. Because of this other styles often perceive these individuals as being cold, aloof or too picky. Your "high C" customers make buying decisions based on research, facts and cost-effectiveness.

Recognizing and understanding the behavioral styles of your prospects and customers will help you to do a better job of meeting their individual needs. Honoring behavioral style differences will help you develop solid relationships with your customers, resulting in higher retention and sales. These solid relationships will set you apart from your competitors and serve as magnets for attracting new business.

SHOW GRATITUDE TO
KEEP YOUR VOLUNTEERS

If organizations expect people to carve out time from their hectic schedules to serve as volunteers and board members, they need to recognize that the most valuable gifts have no price tag on them. The true value of someone's time and talents are measured by the joy and fulfillment they feel when they know that their help has been worthwhile. In order to build loyalty with volunteers, organizations need to reinforce these feelings through proper recognition.

Volunteers need to be treated as the professionals they are. Treat them with the respect you would give a fellow employee. Assign clear titles, job descriptions and schedules. Be sure to communicate realistic expectations of their responsibilities.

Be creative in offering fringe benefits to recognize their gifts of time and talent. Benefits may include:

♦ VIP parking passes

♦ Escort service to the parking lot in the evenings

♦ Reserved seating for institutional activities or events

♦ Complimentary passes or discounts on tickets to special events, dinners and other programs

♦ Snack foods and beverages during meetings

Volunteer recognition needs to be planned and well organized. Thanks given carelessly will take the wind out of volunteers' sails and their enthusiasm will be replaced with apathy. Every volunteer should receive a written "Thank You" for his or her involvement. Whether a typed letter or personal note, the time you spend putting your thanks into words is the sincerest form of recognition.

Each letter should include:

♦ the reason for your gratitude.

♦ specific mention of the project or area the volunteer helped with.

♦ a description of how your organization has benefited from the volunteer's efforts.

♦ a sincere closing reaffirming the volunteer's impor-tance to the organization.

- a signature by the appropriate person (development director, board president, CEO, executive director).

Here are some tips for building loyalty with your volunteers and board members:

- Remember to say "thank you" OFTEN!
- Schedule meetings far enough in advance so that busy board members can get them on their schedules.
- Let board members do their job and don't ask them to do things that go against their professional ethics.
- Hold an appreciation luncheon, dinner or outing for board members at least once a year.
- Answer any questions they may have in a timely manner.
- Treat all board members alike.
- Thank them again for the time they have given you once they leave the board.

Volunteers are the life-blood of nonprofit organizations. They need to be treated as customers and rewarded for their service. When volunteers feel valued and appreciated, they will continue to serve the needs of the organization. They will also prove invaluable in recruiting other volunteers.

WHAT IF YOU DON'T HAVE ANY CUSTOMERS?

Even though you may never meet your company's external customers, you can still make a positive impression on those customers by the way you do your job. Remember, the customer service chain in your organization is only as strong as its weakest link. Each and every employee plays a role in building customer loyalty.

While you are working on tasks and providing service for your internal customers, you need to focus on the needs of the external customers. Ask yourself, "Am I doing what's easiest for me or what's best for the customer?" Many of the actions you take will make a difference to the customers' perceptions of how the company treats them.

Your internal customer service can be as simple as transferring a customer's telephone call to another employee. Let's say a call comes into your department and that call needs to be transferred to another department. The employee in the other department is now your internal customer. If you are required to provide information to another department, such as a billing address from a customer for an employee in the accounts receivable department—that employee is your customer.

Anybody for whom you take a phone message is your customer. Anybody who relies on the way that you do your job is your customer. Make a list of all of the people you touch during the course of the day via phone, email, written or face-to-face communications. These are your customers. Essentially, your customer is anybody who benefits from the way you do your work or suffers if it's done poorly. Identify all your internal customers.

You need to understand that when you help your colleagues to do their jobs more successfully, it not only helps the organization, it also helps you. Your co-workers need to be treated as your primary customers. In fact, they need to be treated like VIPs. Evaluate how your internal customers perceive you. How approachable are you? Do you make it easy for co-workers to request information from you or ask for your help with a project? Do you make eye contact with people when they walk up to your desk or pass you in the corridor? Do you smile at your co-workers?

If possible, seek opportunities to actually meet some of the external customers. Ask a sales representative if you can accompany him or her on a sales call to give you a better perspective on who the customers are. Invite some external customers to visit your department and share feedback with your team on how it feels to do business with the company. Try to keep a picture of a satisfied customer in your mind when you're doing your job.

INFORMATION TECHNOLOGY (IT) PROFESSIONALS NEED TO PROVIDE CUTTING-EDGE SERVICE

When I speak at major events, I am often approached by men and women who introduce themselves as "I'm just the IT guy" or "I'm just the audiovisual person." *Just??*

Without these individuals, my programs would have crashed and burned!

It used to be that the IT professionals in most organizations were the secret technology men and women who worked in hidden departments only to emerge when an employee's computer crashed or new software needed to be installed. Most of us hardly knew who they were, unless we needed them.

Now, IT professionals are at the forefront of customer service. Everyone in the organization needs them. Every situation is urgent. Software and hardware are changing so rapidly that it leaves employees' heads spinning. The IT professionals have become the very lifeblood of the organization because so much of the operation is dependent on their abilities to keep the computers up and running. They're in high demand.

They're not only in demand with their internal customers, they also have high impact on the external customers. Yet, in many organizations, the IT professionals are not required to participate in customer service or communication skills training.

I was chatting with an IT pro the other day and he said, "I've never received any customer service or communication skills training. All the training I received was in dimly lit rooms staring at computer screens. I get so nervous when I need to meet with employees because I'm not sure how to handle their frustrations or explain things to them."

Here are five ways IT professionals can offer cutting edge service:

1. Recognize that employees and co-workers are your primary customers. The way you interact with each employee profoundly affects the way they are able to do their jobs. This impacts the company's image and relationships with external customers.

2. Eliminate the jargon. Speak in a language that your customer understands. Throwing around technical terms and computer jargon will create barriers between you and your customers. You could be perceived as condescending and cold. Never assume that your customer knows (or wants to know) what you know about your job.

3. Listen carefully. Don't jump to conclusions about your customers' needs until you've completely heard them out. Computer problems cause stress and fear in people who do not have technology training. Sometimes your customer just needs an opportunity to vent his or her frustrations and fears.

4.   Be patient. Most of your customers will need to ask you very basic questions in order to understand how to resolve a computer problem. Take time to explain, and then re-explain until you're confident that your customer fully understands what he or she needs to do.

5.   Follow-up. If your customer had a serious technology problem, or is implementing new software, a follow-up phone call or visit will let your customer know that you sincerely care.

IT professionals are now the front-line customer service reps for many organizations. Technology skills alone are not enough to equip them to succeed in their jobs. These men and women handle high-stress and high-impact situations many times each day. They need to have the skills to diffuse anger, communicate change, explain procedures and build solid relationships with co-workers and external customers.

EVERYONE AT WORK IS ON THE SAME TEAM

Every time a customer contacts your company, he or she doesn't care what your title is, what your job responsibilities are or what department you're in. Frankly, all your customer really wants to know is, "Are you willing to help?"

The words most dreaded by customers are, "That's not my job. You'll have to talk to someone in (name the department here)." But even if you aren't the person who will ultimately resolve that customer's issue, you're making a lasting impression just by the way you handle that interaction. No matter what your job, you are the company and everyone who works there is all one team. That's the way your customer sees it.

Research shows that 68 percent of customers who stop doing business with a company leave because of an attitude of indifference by a single employee. That person could be a CEO, manager, supervisor, human resource director or any employee because everyone within the organization is part of a customer service chain. If anyone in the chain weakens the link, the whole chain goes down—taking customer and employee loyalty with it.

Companies will continue to kiss their customers goodbye unless they start treating the causes of poor customer service and stop treating only its symptoms. Companies will lose customers and employees in record numbers unless executives evaluate their companies' culture to identify root causes of their retention problems. Failing to have a policy of customer and employee loyalty is one of those causes.

The #1 loyalty killer is the difference between a customer's expectations and his or her actual experience. Often, the worst offenders are CEOs and upper managers who do not give their employees the same caring service they expect the employees to deliver to the external customers. However, attitudes improve dramatically when employees see the CEO and top managers demonstrating great customer service skills, regardless of their department.

Many companies provide customer service training for call center employees but not for employees in other departments. Customer service training needs to start at the top and be available to all employees. CEOs and upper managers must realize that their primary customers are their employees.

Companies earn loyalty by consistently exceeding expectations through outstanding customer service. This can only be achieved when employees in every department are held accountable for their internal and external customer service skills.

TEAMWORK IS THE
FOUNDATION OF GREAT SERVICE

I frequently hear from managers who are concerned about employee problems. Here is just a sampling of their comments:

- ♦ "Team members aren't getting along."
- ♦ "Back-room gossip and the rumor mill are running rampant."
- ♦ "There is no open communication."

The problems listed above are common occurrences when there has been a merging of two teams, downsizing, rapid company growth or poor management. They are symptoms of a much bigger issue. An obvious lack of team support can seriously damage a business.

Left unchecked, these problems are sure to escalate. They negatively affect employee morale. Customers can feel the tension in the air when there are problems between employees. If the tension is thick enough, your customers will choose to conduct business elsewhere. At the very least, most customers will feel uncomfortable when employees are clearly unhappy.

Here are some tips on how you can bolster team spirit and help create an environment where employees support one another:

- ♦ You don't need to like everyone on the team but you do need to respect their personality and style differences. Rather than judging your co-workers and being quick to notice their faults, take stock of how your own attitude impacts the rest of the team.

- ♦ Provide clear communication and direction for other members of your team. Your co-workers need clearly defined goals and expectations so they can visualize how their job responsibilities fit into the big picture. They also need to understand the roles of other team members.

♦ Meet with employees in your own department and other areas whose work is impacted by the way you do your job. You will build understanding and empathy by asking each other the following questions during these meetings:

- *What does a typical workday look like for you? Describe some of the challenges you face.*

- *How does the way I do my job make your job easier?*

- *How does the way I do my job make your job more difficult?*

- *What would you like me to do differently?*

♦ Encourage balanced participation. This is called shared power and it's the most important aspect of effective teamwork. Everyone's view is respected and accepted without judgment. Every member of the team needs to feel powerful in the sense that he or she can make a difference or can make something happen.

♦ Schedule team improvement meetings on a regular basis. Get the team together and ask them to identify all their strengths. Then ask them to identify all the barriers that are preventing them from working effectively as a team. Focus on issues, not people or personalities. Once they've identified the barriers, they can prioritize them.

♦ Encourage employees to focus on a solution-oriented approach to overcoming the barriers and issues that are causing team problems. Involve the whole team in identifying not only the solutions, but also how to implement them. Solution-oriented brainstorming creates team energy and a sense of ownership in the success of the whole team.

When employees get along and work toward positive solutions, an environment of positive teamwork follows. It takes teamwork to deliver great customer service. Your customers will feel the difference and enjoy doing business with your company.

TAKE TIME TO PRAISE YOUR CO-WORKERS

Have you ever found yourself wishing for an occasional pat on the back? If so, you're not alone. It's only natural to want some credit for your hard work. One of the most common complaints in the workplace is about a lack of recognition or acknowledgment for a job well done.

Don't rely on your boss for recognition. Not all bosses are trained to be effective managers. Some are too busy or stressed out to take time to praise their employees. Recognition is a two-way street. It may be that the reason no one verbalizes their appreciation for the work that you do is because they feel unappreciated themselves. How easy it is to slip into the mindset that if nobody does anything for me, I'm certainly not going to do it for others!

That cycle has to stop somewhere, and it might as well be with you. When was the last time you gave any kind of positive recognition to your boss, your co-workers or the employees who report to you? Have you recently delivered a sincere, heart-felt compliment that had no strings attached to it? Employees need that kind of emotional support in their jobs in order to feel fulfilled in their work.

You need to take time to praise co-workers who have done a great job. I once worked at a company where we had business cards that read, "Great Job," "Outstanding Job," "Exceptionally Outstanding Job." There was a place to fill in the name of the employee and your name. We could hand them out to any employee who we felt deserved the praise. It was easy to observe the pride and happiness in the faces of the recipients of these cards. They felt honored that someone had recognized the fact that they had done their job well.

Sometimes employees get so competitive that they feel that saying something nice to a co-worker would be giving up some of that edge they need in order to get ahead, or they only say something nice because they want something.

Cooperation builds success. No employees today are independent of their co-workers. No one can succeed alone, no matter how great his or her ability. Business today is more than ever a question of cooperation. People will grant your requests if you appeal to their self-interest. Keep in mind that co-workers are your internal customers. They may be in some other department, employees in your own area, or your direct supervisor.

Maybe you've always thought of them as co-workers, or as people you work with rather than for, but make no mistake— these are your primary customers.

School Parents Are Customers, Too

John Baracy, Scottsdale, Arizona, Unified School District superintendent, made improving customer service—with the parent considered the "customer"—a top priority during his first two years on the job.

He attracted national attention by renaming the district receptionist "the director of first impressions." Another key district official has the title "director of exceptional customer experiences." It may sound a little far-fetched, but Baracy has hit the nail on the head. Poor customer service has contributed to declining enrollment in public and private schools alike.

Take, for example, several families in my community who moved their children to a public school because they were fed up with dealing with a rude, indifferent receptionist in the front office at the private school their children had previously attended. They had originally enrolled their children in the Christian school because the parents thought it offered a safe, nurturing environment that fostered kindness and respect. Their illusions were quickly shattered by the treatment they received anytime they needed to deal with the school receptionist.

This receptionist would act annoyed and put out whenever parents requested information or materials. She carried on personal phone conversations and ignored busy parents who were waiting to be buzzed into the locked lobby, even if they were arriving to attend a school-sponsored meeting. She often failed to return phone calls in a timely manner. Her negative attitude and penchant for gossip created many morale problems with faculty and staff.

Enrollment in school districts around the country continues to decline. Parents have many educational choices: traditional public schools, publicly funded charter schools, private and parochial schools, and even home schools. Teachers, principals and receptionists who treat parents shabbily run the risk of driving them away.

Baracy is interested in developing a "secret parent" initiative. He would model the "parent" after the "secret shoppers" commonly used by department stores to gauge how responsive and helpful the retail staff is to customers. The secret parent would report on his or her experience with the school officials.

Historically, excellent customer service has not been a priority at many public schools. It took legislative reforms of the 1990s such as open enrollment to hammer home its importance.

Some school administrators understand this and some district officials, incredibly, still don't.

In order for schools to continue to grow and thrive, it's essential that school administrators, principals, office staff and even teachers recognize that parents and students are their primary customers. Schools need to create and maintain a customer service culture. All employees must realize that they work for the customer, and their job is to ensure the ultimate satisfaction of all customers (internal as well as external customers). Every other task is of secondary importance.

WHAT KIND OF CUSTOMER ARE YOU?

Customers frequently complain about the poor service they receive from store clerks and cashiers. But is it always the clerk's fault? Many employees are struggling to stay positive because customers are treating them more rudely these days.

Customer service is a two-way street. We need to ask ourselves, "How are we treating the people who are providing us with service in the malls, shops and restaurants where we do business?"

Especially during busy shopping seasons, try to keep in mind that most of these employees are trying to do the best they can. Many are over-worked and underpaid.

Here are some tips that will help you spread a positive spirit and feel good about the positive difference you make:

+ Allow enough time for your shopping so you don't feel rushed.

+ Smile at the clerks and wait-staff, even if they don't reciprocate.

+ Show empathy to individuals who are clearly under pressure.

- ◆ Catch the clerks doing things right and compliment them.

- ◆ Thank everyone with whom you do business.

Many of us have been so disillusioned by poor service that we don't give even the caring employees a chance to deliver good service.

TURN ON YOUR CHARM TO GET GREAT SERVICE

Have you ever noticed that some people seem to get great service everywhere they go? This isn't just plain luck. It's the result of having the ability to turn on their charm. If you want to receive good service, you need to be pleasant and charming to the service provider. Turning on your charm will make the other person feel appreciated and want to give you more. Graciousness and charm are the keys to being treated well. Most service providers are grateful when their customers have treated them with kindness.

The easiest way to get what you want is to make a pleasant request and deliver it with a sincere smile. Manners are also very important. You'll be more likely to get your requests met when you use the word "please" along with a gracious smile, eye contact, and a warm tone of voice.

Charm is the art of having an attractive personality. While some people seem to be natural charmers, it is a skill that can be acquired and honed through practice and patience. As with any skill, the more you practice, the better you will become. Effort and careful attention to the needs and desires of others will ensure that charm becomes a permanent part of your character. Charming people are more likely to be successful than their less captivating counterparts. To be charming, not only do you have to show yourself in a good light, but you have to make other people feel good about themselves as well. It works, and it's really simple to be charming.

Here are five tips to help you to turn on your charm:

1. Greet everyone you meet with enthusiasm. Treat each person like an old friend who is special.

2. Pay careful attention when the other person is speaking. Show that you are sincerely interested in what they're sharing. When people feel listened to, they feel happier and they'll equate feeling good to talking to you.

3. Be generous with "thank you's." Gratitude shows others that you appreciate what they've done and they'll be more drawn to you.

4. Show people they impress you with a sincere compliment. If you like something or someone, find a creative way to say it and say it immediately. If you wait too long, it may be viewed as insincere. If you notice that someone is putting a lot of effort into something, compliment it, even if you feel that there is room for improvement.

5. Never over-explain anything. Doing this simply confirms a lack of self-esteem, or shows you don't trust that others have understood your point. Or it may be perceived as arrogance because it demonstrates a feeling on your behalf that your listeners cannot think for themselves.

Being charming is about making others feel good around you. If you look around at people who hold high-level positions, they usually have a quick smile, know how to talk to people in a professional but friendly manner, and can very easily sway people to their point of view. They have earned their position by impressing the right people at the right time.

Being charming has become part of their personality. A charming person is one who draws others to them because they emit warmth and confidence. These are both important things to have when you're talking about careers. But when you learn how to turn on your charm, you will also be rewarded with better service.

SELF-ASSESSMENT
ARE YOU DELIGHTING YOUR CUSTOMERS?

Each of us has the opportunity every day to build loyalty by exceeding the expectations of our internal and external customers. Caring, personalized service builds positive relationships, one customer at a time. Because this type of service is rare these days, customers are delighted when they receive it, and their loyalty to the company grows.

1. I understand that my co-workers are also my customers and that we are all part of a customer service chain.
    True   False

2. I take ownership of my customers' problems and do everything possible to avoid having to transfer their call to another area.
    True   False

3. I use my customer's name in every conversation.
    True   False

4. I listen very carefully to what my customers are telling me, so I can clearly understand their needs and feelings.
    True   False

5. When my customers are upset, I sincerely try to empathize with their concerns and try to put myself in their place.
    True   False

6. I always assume that my customers are being honest.
    True   False

7. I try to be flexible to meet the needs of my customers.
    True   False

8. I try to do what is best for my customers, not what is easiest for me.
    True   False

9. I smile a lot, even when I am on the phone, because I know that my customers can "hear" a smile.
True   False

10. I look for ways to build loyalty even when I can't provide the service that my customer has requested.
True   False

11. When I need to transfer my customer's call to another area, I contact the other employee and explain my customer's problem so they do not need to repeat it.
True   False

12. I follow up with every customer who was upset or had a complex problem.
True   False

13. I stop what I'm doing to actively listen when co-workers or customers are speaking to me.
True   False

14. I follow up with co-workers to let them know the outcome of the service they started and needed to send to me for completion.
True   False

15. I add my personal "signature" to every customer interaction.
True   False

16. I look for ways to spread a positive customer service spirit.
True   False

17. I ask myself with every customer, "If this were me, what would I expect?"
True   False

18. I always thank my customer for calling, no matter what the service request.
True   False

19. I take time to explain all information carefully, without using jargon or assuming that the customer understands the details of our business.
True   False

20. I frequently compliment my co-workers for a job well done--in front of other people.
True   False

21. I make a sincere effort to remember personal details about my customers such as birthdays, children's names, their jobs and accomplishments.
True   False

22. I treat my customers with respect and do not become defensive, even when they are angry.
True   False

23. I understand that my customers' time is extremely valuable, so I do everything to provide them with fast, seamless service.
True   False

24. I am willing to go the extra mile for each of my customers to delight them with service that exceeds their expectations.
True   False

25. I look for opportunities to thank my customers every chance I get.
True   False

If you had **20 to 25 'True'** responses, CONGRATULATIONS! You are consistently delighting your customers and building customer loyalty.

If you had **15 to 19 'True'** responses, you're on your way and you have an opportunity to improve your service skills.

If you had **fewer than 15 'True'** responses, you may need some extra customer service skill coaching.

CHAPTER 3

WHY CUSTOMERS LEAVE

Your most unhappy customers are your greatest source of learning.

— Bill Gates

ARE YOU KISSING YOUR CUSTOMERS GOODBYE?

Take time to assess the way you interact with your customers. Are your actions making them want to do business with your company? Or, are you kissing your customers goodbye?

Now, more than ever before, it is important to identify the reasons your customers leave. While there are some reasons that we cannot control, such as lower demands for the product or the tight economy, research shows that 91 percent of customers leave for reasons that we can control.

While conducting a workshop at Northwestern Mutual, I asked a group of 20 top-notch customer service employees this question, "As the customer, have you ever decided to stop doing business with a company due to poor service?"

They all answered, "Yes."

Then I asked, "Did you leave because of the way you were treated by one employee?"

Again, they responded with a unanimous, "Yes."

Then, I asked them to tell me how that employee behaved. Here were their responses. The employee:

- ◆ was rude.
- ◆ ignored me.
- ◆ had a negative attitude.
- ◆ was impatient with me.
- ◆ hung up on me.
- ◆ got defensive and started blaming me.
- ◆ gave me the wrong info.
- ◆ bounced me all over the company.
- ◆ didn't tell me about the hidden charges.
- ◆ was not knowledgeable about the products.
- ◆ wouldn't listen.
- ◆ had preconceived ideas about the situation, was close-minded.
- ◆ was unprofessional.
- ◆ put me on interminable "hold."
- ◆ sent me to the wrong department.
- ◆ did not understand other areas of the company.
- ◆ provided no follow-through.
- ◆ did not return my phone message or emails.

- did not speak clearly enough for me to understand.

- was not willing to be accountable for my service request.

This list by no means represents all the reasons that customers leave. But the behaviors of so-called service providers in a variety of industries caused this group to take their business elsewhere.

Take time to review these items and then review your own actions. Is there anything that can change? As fuel, food and other prices continue to skyrocket, your customers are going to be far more selective about the companies where they choose to take their business.

Every time you lose a customer, you lose a lifetime opportunity of profitability with that individual. They may cause other customers to leave if they complain to their friends, family and colleagues. Every customer counts. They are the very reason you have your job. The more customers you keep, the more job stability you have.

Most Customers Leave for Reasons We Can Control

Customers leave businesses for many different reasons. When you review the percentages listed below, you'll see that nine percent of customers leave for reasons over which you have little or no control.

- **1 percent die**

- **3 percent move away.**
  People are on the move. It's estimated in the real estate industry that the average length of stay in a newly purchased home is only four years. Business-to-business

customers are also on the move. They are frequently switching employers.

◆ **5 percent develop new relationships.**
Customers are influenced by their family, friends and colleagues. If trusted friends recommend a different vendor, they may talk your customers into taking their business elsewhere.

Ninety-one percent of customers leave businesses for reasons related to poor customer service.

◆ **9 percent leave for competitive reasons.**
Your customers are continually shopping for value. This is basically an equation comprised of the following elements:

VALUE = Fair Prices + Quality Products + *Caring Service*

Today's consumers are very educated and the Internet has made it easy to compare businesses. It is quite likely that your customers will be able to find other businesses that offer comparable prices and products. More often than not, it is caring service that will set you apart from your competitors.

◆ **14 percent are dissatisfied with the product or service purchased.**
Customer dissatisfaction is frequently the result of over-promising and under-delivering by someone within your organization. The promise can be product-related or it can be as simple as promising a customer that a call will be returned at 2:00 p.m., and, instead, the return call takes place at 2:30 p.m.

◆ **68 percent are treated poorly by a single employee!**
One negative interaction with an employee may be the reason a customer could choose to leave. The employee

who delivered the poor service could be the CEO, a sales representative, a human resources manager, or the mailroom clerk. Everyone in the organization, regardless of job title or position, is part of a customer service chain. If anyone breaks his or her link in the chain, it ultimately hurts the quality of service provided to external customers.

TEN REASONS
YOUR CUSTOMERS COMPLAIN

Any employee in your organization can be the cause of your customers' complaints.

1. Your customer was made to feel embarrassed because he or she was responsible for the mistake.

2. Your customer was treated rudely.

3. A promise was made but not kept.

4. Your customer's honesty or integrity was questioned.

5. No one was willing to take ownership of your customer's problem.

6. An employee acted like he or she didn't care ("It's not my job" syndrome).

7. Everyone was too busy or unavailable to help your customer resolve his or her problem.

8. Your customer was told he or she had no reason to be angry.

9. Your customer was told that he or she was to blame.

10. Your customer's time was wasted.

YOU'RE ABOUT TO LOSE A CUSTOMER: EARLY WARNING SIGNS

Many companies do not know that a customer is leaving until it's too late. But there are early warning systems that may tell you if customers are getting ready to jump ship. Here are some red flags that can indicate whether a customer is going to remain loyal or head to the competition:

Squeaky Wheels

The most obvious sign of an unhappy customer is the customer complaint. The initial problem is only the beginning. Your customer might also be unhappy with the way the problem was resolved. That adds another layer to the interaction. Companies should track complaints from the first call to the resolution, and make sure that customers emerge from the process happier than when they entered. Also watch for recurring problems. If your company is receiving numerous complaints about the same product or service, then there is a good chance you're going to lose customers.

Product Returns

When a customer returns a product, it is another early warning sign that a customer may be ready to give up on a company and start looking to its competitors. Not all the reasons for returning products are negative. Sometimes your customer makes a mistake or orders the wrong size. Good customer service employees keep a close eye on returns, and they track the reasons products are returned. Watch for trends—product defects, misinformation during the sales process, poor packaging for shipping, etc. Most can be fixed quite easily to prevent customer dissatisfaction.

Silence

When customers are complaining and returning products, at least they're in touch with the business. No contact at all can be a warning signal. If a customer fails to respond to a customer survey or return your calls, the business has cause to worry about customer retention.

Slow Pay

A lack of response can take many forms. For instance, if customers are taking longer to pay bills, companies should treat the situation as more than a receivables issue. There may be issues with your products or services that caused them to put you at the bottom of the pay list.

DRAIN THE SWAMP INSTEAD OF FIGHTING THE ALLIGATORS

Think of customer complaints as alligators. If several customers complain about the same thing, you've got a swamp full of alligators. When this occurs, it's time to drain the swamp. Get rid of the problem that's attracting the gators.

* * *

My son needed a haircut so I took him to a local salon. After waiting only a few minutes, I said to the receptionist, "It's freezing in here."

She replied, "I know. Our customers are always complaining that it's too cold."

"Why don't you turn down the air conditioning?" I asked.

"The owner likes it this way."

* * *

I went to my bank to make a deposit. All the pens attached to the chains were out of ink. I had to wait several minutes to get an employee's attention so I could request a pen. I said, "All the pens are dry."

"I know," she said. "Our pens are always running out of ink."

* * *

The climate of the building needs to be set with the comfort of the customers in mind. If your customers complain about being too hot or cold, adjust the settings.

Banking customers need pens. When they're chained to the counter, it's a message to the customer that he or she cannot be trusted. Banks should put out a whole tray of pens with the company name, web address and phone number on them. That way, if a customer does take one along, it will provide that customer with easy access to important information about the bank.

Think about the times you've complained about an inconvenience and an employee responded, "I know. Our customers complain about that all the time."

If you know that something is annoying your customers, change it. Otherwise, they will eventually go away. Customers are too valuable to ignore their feedback. There's no point in listening to your customer's complaint if nothing is going to be done to fix the problem. Dealing with the same complaints over and over wastes a considerable amount of employee time that could be better-spent building positive relationships with customers.

MISTAKES DON'T DRIVE CUSTOMERS AWAY—PEOPLE DO

Customers generally do not decide to stop doing business with a company because a mistake was made. They stop doing business because of the way the relationship was handled. People, not mistakes, drive customers away. Mistakes happen in business all the time. Customers don't demand perfection but they do expect to be treated with respect and kindness when a mistake does occur.

Listed below are twelve of the most common causes of poor service. Notice that nine of the causes involve employee behavior toward customers or management's behavior toward the employees:

1. Poorly trained or ineffective managers

2. Uncaring employees

3. Differences in the way the company thinks customers want to be treated and what the customers really want

4. Poor or limited employee training

5. Poor handling of customer complaints

6. Management not treating employees as customers

7. Lack of recognition for employees when they demonstrate positive attitudes and provide great service

8. No solid customer service philosophy within the company

9. Employees are not empowered to provide good service, take responsibility or make decisions to go the extra mile for the customer

10. Negative attitudes of employees toward customers

11. Inadequate staff, phone systems, computer software or other necessary resources

12. Broken promises

Don't wait for your customers to complain. Instead of asking your customers what they like about the service they've received, ask them, "What are we doing that's irritating you?" Then be prepared to receive an earful of complaints, ideas and suggestions.

It is precisely this kind of customer feedback that many companies choose to ignore or make excuses for. When you honor this kind of honest feedback from your customers, you will learn how to avoid the mistakes that irritate your customers. You'll also gain powerful tools to rise above the competition.

The reason most customers leave is because they are frustrated with the employee who handled their complaint. A complaint offers a wonderful opportunity to build a positive relationship with that customer but many employees are ill equipped to handle difficult circumstances.

Companies need to invest in training employees to build rapport with customers even in the most difficult circumstances. Loyalty-focused employees listen carefully and take action to fix the problems.

CAUTION: ROBOTS AT WORK

I stood in line at the grocery store behind a 5-year-old girl and her mother. As they approached the cashier, the little girl looked up at her mom and said, "Paper or plastic, Mommy?"

All the customers, including me, cracked up laughing. But when the laughter subsided, I overheard a number of side conversations taking place. People began chatting with one another about their awful customer service experiences. The more they shared, the more annoyed they sounded.

That little comment from an innocent child was a reflection of a big problem I call "robotism." Robotism occurs when customers are treated like numbers instead of human beings.

When evaluating the quality of your organization's customer service, it's important to focus considerable energy on the human side of the business. Look for ways to shift your service delivery from being task-oriented to relationship-oriented.

Task-oriented service focuses on getting the job done quickly and efficiently, "Thank you, have a nice day. Next!" But it does not add the human touch and does nothing to build positive, lasting relationships with your customers.

To build loyalty, emphasis must to be placed on building rapport and trust through careful listening, empathy and personal touches such as using the customer's name. It is the customer's perception of his experience with your organization that can create or destroy loyalty. Evaluate the quality of service through the eyes of your customers.

THE CUSTOMER SERVICE OBSTACLE COURSE

Have you ever noticed how some companies seem to go out of their way to place obstacles between their customers and great service?

Here are examples of just a few of the customer service barriers I've bumped into during the past month:

Signage that gives orders to customers

"You must stand behind the line until you're called."

"Absolutely NO PARKING."

"Commercial Banking Customers ONLY."

Tip:

Harsh words like "should," "must," and "only" are likely to offend your customers. Your signs need to include words like "welcome," "please," and "thank you."

Sometimes humor can be used to soften the message on a sign:

On a maternity room door: "Push. Push. Push."
In a non-smoking area: "If we see smoke, we will assume you're on fire and take appropriate action."

Inconvenient Business Hours

One local library locks the book return drop-box during the hours that the library is open. This means customers have to find a parking place, get the kids out of the car, lock it and traipse into the library just to return a book.

Here's another barrier: The post office has a sign by the mailbox rental area that reads, "Box mail is available for pick up after 10:30 a.m." Located next to that area is a service window for mailbox renters. The sign on that door reads, "Mailbox service window is open 8 to 9 a.m."

In other words, you can only pick up your mail after 10:30 a.m., but if you need to pick up a package that was too large for your mailbox, you have to come back the following day to catch the service window hours.

Tip:

Obstacles that waste a customer's time will eventually drive that customer away. Review your business hours to see if there is an opportunity to expand them or eliminate outdated rules.

Unknowledgeable Employees

While visiting my health club the other day, I asked for some basic information about hours and pool rules at the customer service desk. The employee looked up at me and said, "You're asking the wrong guy ... I haven't got a clue!" He was also clueless about who could provide the answers.

Tip:

It is totally unforgivable when employees are unable to answer the basic questions asked by your customers. Just because employees have gone through training, don't assume that they remember everything they've been taught. Quiz employees on a regular basis to make sure they know the answers to frequently asked questions.

TOOTHPICK SHATTERS FIRST IMPRESSION

At first I was impressed with the manager of a local grocery store. When he noticed a lot of customers waiting in line, he raced to the front of the store and opened a check-out lane.

My impression of him changed dramatically as I took my place in his line. He didn't smile at a single customer. He couldn't, because the toothpick he was chewing on would have dropped out of his mouth.

Soon, I became fascinated with the toothpick. While he was chomping away, that little piece of lumber was jumping around his mouth like a nervous grasshopper. Furthermore, in his attempt to be efficient, he rushed his customers through his lane and appeared annoyed when they didn't pay for their groceries with the same sense of urgency.

When it was my turn, I smiled sweetly and said, "The toothpick doesn't convey a very professional image for a manager."

He glared at me and said, "Well, ma'am, I'm sorry if it offends you."

I replied, "It doesn't offend me in the least but it certainly lowers your professional credibility."

Then I smiled once more and started to walk away. He looked at me, whispered "Thanks" and quietly removed the toothpick from his mouth. Then he looked directly at his next customer and gave her a big smile.

HOW TO DRIVE AWAY A CUSTOMER IN 30 SECONDS FLAT

It only takes one employee 30 seconds to destroy a customer relationship that has taken months or even years to develop.

In a traditional sales environment, a sales representative will make ten phone calls just to schedule a single appointment. And just because an appointment has been scheduled, there's no guarantee that the prospect will actually follow through with the meeting. No relationship has been established yet. If there is a time conflict for the prospective customer, he or she may be likely to cancel at the last minute.

A sales representative must meet with as many as ten separate individuals to get one prospective customer. A prospect is not someone who simply looks over the company's marketing materials. A prospect is someone who has a real need for the products or services your company offers, and can afford them.

It takes three qualified prospects to make a single sale. This sales process can take months or even years to complete. For example, a financial representative called to encourage me to purchase a life insurance policy from the company she represents. We met a couple of times. I liked her and the products she sold, but I just wasn't ready to purchase. She stayed in touch with me about once a quarter to give me product updates and maintain the relationship. Two years after her initial contact, I finally decided to buy a policy through her.

As a trainer and consultant, I've had the privilege of observing customer service operations in all type of industries. I've heard phone conversations that were handled so poorly that they drove away long-term customers. I've witnessed customers stomping out of businesses, vowing never to return because they were so disgusted by the poor service they had just received.

One single customer interaction or phone call can destroy a customer relationship. That's why it's so critical for everyone in the organization to take ownership of the customer's needs. Excellent customer service requires that you set goals to personally guarantee that each of your customers leaves happy.

EIGHT DEADLY CUSTOMER SERVICE SINS

There are common behaviors that will drive customers away. These service sins are committed by individual employees and are often a result of poor training and negative attitudes. Careful observation by everyone will help you identify which types of service sins are being committed in your company.

Here are eight of the most common sins to watch for:

1. **Apathy**: Or the "I don't give a rip about you or my job attitude."

2. **Brush Off**: Finding ways to get rid of customers by transferring their calls or using negative phrases such as, "We can't do that for you in this department."

3. **Coldness**: Impatience, curtness, even hostility toward customers or co-workers.

4. **Condescension**: A patronizing attitude and using a customer's first name without their permission. Using jargon and acronyms that your customer doesn't understand. Blaming the customer for the problem.

5. **Robotism**: "Have-a-nice-day-next" treatment where customers feel like nothing more than numbers. (I like to call this one "Paper or Plastic!")

6. **Rulebook**: Using company guidelines as excuses for not providing service even when an employee knows they can be flexible.

7. **Run-Around**: Sending the customer on a wild goose chase because no one is willing to take ownership of his or her problem.

8. **Tune Out**: Not focusing 100 percent on the person who is speaking; judging before you've heard the person out; not asking questions to verify that you understand what was said, and not giving appropriate responses.

The best way to eliminate customer service sins is by making everyone in your organization part of the customer service improvement team. Involve your employees in finding ways to eliminate your company's service sins.

Ask each member of your team to make a list of the sins (not the names of the people committing them) they observe during a one-week period. Bring everyone's list to a staff meeting and, as a team, rank the service sins, with #1 being the most frequently observed. Then brainstorm ways service can be improved to eliminate the sins. (HINT: Taking ownership of attitudes!)

FOUL LANGUAGE TAINTS LOYALTY

We attended the funeral of a friend last spring. I brought our young son, Dave, along because the elderly woman who had passed away adored him. Since it was Memorial Day weekend, my plan was to head home after the funeral but Dave asked me if we could drive in the funeral procession and go to the cemetery. After a few minutes, I agreed. He had been to funerals before but never to the cemetery. I thought it would be a good experience for him.

Dave enjoyed the ride across town, especially the part where you get to go through red lights. We sang along to the radio and chatted as we drove. When we arrived at the entrance to the cemetery, I turned off the radio and explained that now we needed to be quiet and respectful. It was a beautiful day and we had all the windows open.

As we headed toward our friend's final resting place, the silence was shattered by a cemetery employee yelling obscenities at another employee who apparently had been telling the people in our procession to park in the wrong place. Profanities spewed from this guy's mouth for all to hear. Although I knew it was too late, I quickly closed the car windows so Dave wouldn't hear the words.

My initial shock turned to anger. This one individual tainted the whole beautiful service through his careless choice of words. It was an incredible show of disrespect toward the family of the deceased and offensive to all who attended. I pulled up next to him in my car and sharply told him to cut out the foul language.   He apologized, but the damage had been done.

* * *

I once took an outfit to a dry cleaning store. The outfit belongs to my mom and I wasn't sure if it could be dry-cleaned because, apparently, she had cut the care tags off. I asked the clerk if she knew. She looked for the tags and I told her they were missing. She exclaimed, "Well, that sucks. It was stupid to cut out the tags."

I picked up the garment and walked out. I have no desire to do business with anyone who uses foul language. If it's used in front of any customer, it's wrong. If it's used in front of a child, it's disgusting.

Customers deserve to be treated with respect at all times. It is never acceptable to use any profanity or even crude language that is acceptable on television. When employees use inappropriate language that can be heard by a customer, it's a sign of disrespect.

Foul language demonstrates to the customer that the employee lacks maturity and professionalism. It's a sure way to offend individuals and it lowers their ability to trust the integrity of the entire organization.

DISENGAGED EMPLOYEES DON'T CARE

You can bet that quarterback Kyle Orton cared deeply about his team and was committed to winning when he lead the Chicago Bears to eight consecutive victories in 2007. You know he was motivated when he won 10 games as a starter in his first NFL season. The team rewarded his motivation by bumping him to the position of third string quarterback. Orton was benched halfway through the season in the middle of a game, because the team was "struggling." I wondered if he would continue to care enough to do his best for the team once he got the chance to play again.

Now I'm no expert on football but I was struck by how similar Kyle Orton's situation is to loyal employees who have worked hard for a company for years, only to be bumped when a new "star" is hired. They look on from the sidelines and feel unappreciated for their loyalty to the company. There are many employees who show up on time every day, treat their co-workers with respect and deliver quality work, only to be taken for granted by their managers.

The Gallup Organization, famous for its research, estimates that 70 percent of employees are "disengaged," meaning they're no longer committed to the company. It's evident in positions from executive officers to front-line employees. This "I don't care" attitude is hurting businesses in a big way. What's going on? Why all the apathy? It could be that the wrong employees are being rewarded.

Most organizations want to blame employee apathy on wages and benefits, but they actually do not play a big role in why people stop caring about their jobs. The overwhelming majority of employees stop caring because of the way they are treated every day. Surveys show that lack of appreciation, lack of teamwork and the perception that the company doesn't care about loyal employees are consistently the highest-ranked reasons for low job satisfaction.

Many managers are nice people who manage by negative reinforcement—demonstrated not by what they do but, rather, by what they don't do. Chances are, these same managers are focusing their energy and attention on those employees with behavioral problems. If loyal employees aren't recognized and appreciated for their contributions, they'll be far less motivated to care about the success of the company. Sometimes, even the best employees will go through rough spots but will bounce back with more energy and loyalty when the company stands behind them with clearly defined expectations, quality training and positive feedback.

Gallup estimates that actively disengaged workers in the United States miss 118.3 million more work days per year than their actively engaged counterparts. Harder to measure are their higher healthcare, workers' compensation, and safety costs.

But disengaged employees who show up and simply go through the motions of work cause the biggest problem. It's reflected in everything they don't do and their constant complaints. It's the negative effect their attitudes have on their co-workers and customers. This problem has become so common as to create a new word, "presenteeism."

Gallup found that the cumulative effect of disengaged employees consistently reduces customer loyalty, sales and profit margins. An "I don't care" attitude by employees translates to an "I don't care to do business with you" attitude by customers.

LUNACY IN THE LAP LANE

My husband and I were lounging by the pool at our health club when we were rattled out of our revelry by a commotion in the lap lanes.

For ten minutes or so, we had been chatting while two women were swimming laps in the pool in front of us. They were in separate lanes. One woman was in her mid-40s and the other woman was around 70. Suddenly, the younger woman stopped swimming, and whacked the older swimmer on the shoulder with her Styrofoam kickboard.

She continued hitting the older woman with her kickboard while yelling at her, "You've bumped into me three times! Why don't you watch where you're going?"

She was yelling so loudly that everyone in the pool stopped what they were doing and stared at her. The older woman was shielding herself from the blows and apologizing. "I didn't mean to bump you. I've stayed in my own lane. I'm sorry," she said.

"Well, sorry isn't good enough," the younger woman replied. "I take my swimming seriously, and you should learn the rules." With that, she swam off.

It was like a crazy *Saturday Night Live* episode. Most of the observers were mildly shocked and angered by the woman's behavior. Some found it quite amusing. A few people sitting by the edge of the pool started laughing at the offending woman. Once again she stopped, looked up at the laughing group and said, "Oh, sure, use me as your weekend entertainment, why don't you?"

The kickboard was light and the woman didn't actually hit hard enough to cause physical harm. But the older swimmer was clearly shaken and upset. After a few minutes, she quietly exited the pool and headed indoors.

Regardless of pool rules, there is no question that the younger woman was way out of line. No one wants to belong to a family-oriented health club where this type of behavior is tolerated. I carefully watched the lifeguards and club staff to see if anyone was going to address the issue of inappropriate behavior with the woman who did the hitting. No one did.

One group of club members was so angry about the incident that they wanted the woman's membership revoked. Others talked to the head of the aquatics program and requested that she at least address the issue with the swimmer who did the hitting. The director laughed nervously and said, "I don't know what to say to her. Let's just hope it doesn't happen again."

The health club staff's lack of willingness to act on this matter caused a great deal of frustration with many members. Some threatened to cancel their memberships. As customers of the club, they felt they had a right to expect all members to adhere to the rules of etiquette and courtesy. Their lack of ability to take action in this matter caused the club to lose good members. Ironically, the woman who caused the problem is still there swimming laps as if nothing had happened. I haven't seen the older woman since that day.

Employees need to be trained and empowered to deal with customers who act inappropriately. When the nasty behavior of a single customer is not addressed, it can do considerable damage to the image of a business. It compromises the quality of service that all of the other customers receive. It also lowers the credibility of all employees who are present.

You owe it to your customers to deliver great service in an environment where they feel valued and safe. This means that no behavior that is offensive to other customers can be tolerated. The employees at my health club clearly were ill-equipped to handle this type of situation. Conflict management training is essential for employees who work in organizations where there is considerable interaction between customers.

─────────────────────────────

THESE CUSTOMERS KEEP BUGGING ME

It was 5:30 p.m. and the after-work crowd was stopping by the drycleaner to drop off items in need of cleaning. About this same time, I stopped in to pick up my order. There were clothes piled everywhere.

"Wow," I said. "This is a really busy time of day for you guys."

One employee looked at me and said, "Yeah. I wish all these people would stop coming in. I've got a lot of stuff to do and the customers keep bugging me."

Oops. He said it to the wrong person. Little did he know with whom he was dealing! For the next 10 minutes, I launched into a mini-workshop on building customer loyalty. When I was finished, he smiled sheepishly and said, "I guess I never looked at this job that way. But it's tough to focus on the customers when there's so much to do."

He's right. Everyone is getting busier. With downsizing and hiring freezes, there are simply not enough employees to handle the ever-growing workloads. That's why it's more important than ever to identify your priorities and stick to them.

Here is the simple message I shared with this young, over-worked employee … Remember, relationships come before tasks.

Put Relationship Before Task.

Never view a customer as an interruption of your work. Instead, prioritize your efforts by first completing tasks that build relationships with your customers. Organize your job duties into two columns:

Column 1 - Activities that build customer relationships. For example:

- Greeting customers warmly.
- Listening to customers.
- Opening another cash register when there's a line.
- Answering the phone in 3 rings or less.
- Placing customers on hold for less than 30 seconds.
- Returning customer phone calls promptly.
- Shipping orders within the promised time frame.
- Responding to customer emails.
- Keeping customers updated about product or service changes.
- Quickly resolving customer complaints.

Column 2 - All other tasks, or "stuff" that can be done after the customer's needs have been met. *Hot tip*: You can interrupt these tasks anytime a customer needs your attention! For example:

- Reading emails.
- Filing.
- Preparing invoices.
- Writing reports.
- Conducting inventory.

- Sorting mail.

- Preparing a report.

- Making copies.

Loyalty Leader® Rules for Relationship Before Task:

Customers are absolutely the most important people in the company.

- The most important job you have is to make your customers happy.

- You are not doing your customers a favor when you provide service for them.

- Your customers are not dependent upon you. They have many other choices.

- Your customers will reward great service with business. Their business means you have a job!

WHY CUSTOMERS GET ANGRY EVEN WHEN YOU'RE NICE

Dealing with customers is one of the most stressful jobs around. Customers can be unpredictable, impatient and even downright rude at times. But it's not entirely their fault. Overall, customers are fed up with receiving poor service practically everywhere they go. Often, they're ready to take their frustrations out on you before you even pick up the phone or greet them. There are a number of reasons why customers get angry even when you're trying to be nice.

Time

What's your most precious commodity? If you're like most people, it's probably time. When dealing with customers you need to keep in mind that one of their most precious assets is time. Whenever customers or co-workers feel that their time has been wasted, they view it as a disservice and loyalty actually decreases. So, it's important to look for ways that you can speed up service and move things along, without making your customers feel rushed.

Exerting a little more effort to ensure clear communication early in the conversation can save time later on. Your customers are very busy people, just like you are. That's why it's important to identify and remove communication barriers. Get together with your team and identify the barriers in your department or company that waste customers' time. You'll be amazed at what you find. It might be the way that the phone transfers are handled. Maybe the voice mail messages are too long or too difficult for customers to navigate.

Past Experiences

Your customers come to you with a history of negative service experiences. It doesn't matter the industry, people are frustrated when they've had to stand in line too long. Many have gotten the run-around where they had to repeat their story multiple times before someone listened. For some they've had situations where their service was never completed to their satisfaction. Customers have a lot of pent-up frustration. Even when you're trying to be very helpful and nice, one negative phrase or word ("I'm sorry sir, we don't do that in this department") can set your customer off.

Language Barriers

In this global marketplace, there are cultural and ethnic language barriers that will come into play. There are also speech barriers such as people who speak too quickly or, people who speak too softly. Some customers may be difficult to understand due to disabilities. You need to learn how to recognize these differences and adapt the way you communicate to make it easier for your customers to understand you. You can also ask your customers to slow down or repeat information without offending them. You simply use "I" language. For example, "Mr. Froemming, could you please repeat your last name for me more slowly so that I can be sure that I pronounce it correctly?"

Phone Systems

Phone systems create tremendous barriers for customers. Customers get offended when they hear a voice mail menu that has 15 options from which to choose. Then they have to listen to the whole thing to find out which button to push in order to speak to a live human being. When they finally get through, the service representative says, "I can't help. I'll need to transfer your call."

If you're the person who handles that transferred call, you're going to be dealing with an angry customer. Your first steps with that customer will need to address their frustration at getting caught in the voice mail nightmare. Even recorded messages can create problems. Martha Stewart stopped doing business with one of her financial agencies because she found their music to be too annoying when she was on hold. That's pretty extreme, but you need to be aware that sometimes recorded messages or music can be offensive to your customers.

Personal Reasons

Sometimes your customers are just upset about something else when they call. Maybe they're going through a difficult time with their marriage or they have a health concern. If you work in the health care or financial industry you will probably deal with more angry customers. Money and health issues create stress for people and are often accompanied by fear. So, let's say you're in the banking industry and you have a customer on the phone who's upset because he received an overdraft notice for his checking account. He's angry because according to his records he is not overdrawn. There's an element of fear involved because it has to do with financial security. It's important to understand that fear will often come across as anger.

These issues don't only affect your external customers. The way that you interact and communicate with your co-workers profoundly impacts the relationships that your company has with its external customers. Keep in mind that your customers may have already had three or four really negative service experiences today alone. Show them empathy and understanding and they'll come around because they'll be relieved to be doing business with someone who cares.

CUSTOMER SILENCE
IS NOT ALWAYS GOLDEN

A customer complaint is a gift. It generally means that a customer cares enough about doing business with your company to give you a second chance. But what if no one's complaining? Is it true that "no news is good news?" Not when it comes to customers.

Silence is not always golden. It's usually the quiet customers who leave. Most unhappy customers don't bother to complain because they don't believe anyone will listen. Or, even if someone does listen, they don't believe anything will change because of their complaint. There are many times that customers experience problems and choose not to say anything about it. So the silences accumulate until they become so frustrated that they quietly look for another place to take their business.

There are different types of quiet customers to consider:

Satisfied Customers

Most businesses assume that the majority of their customers are satisfied because they haven't heard complaints from them. Satisfied often means "neutral" and these customers are keeping one eye open to see if they can find a better place to take their business. The Internet has made it easier than ever to search. Don't settle for satisfied customers. Focus on building loyalty. Loyal customers are more likely to complain because they believe you care enough to fix the problem.

Collectors

These customers are usually very busy and they don't want to waste their time by complaining. So they let the problems collect until they become so frustrated that they unleash their anger when you ask, "How are you doing today?"

Dashers

These customers are very uncomfortable when dealing with conflict so they will avoid it by dashing to a different company that offers similar products or services.

Guessers

These customers are the ones who say to themselves, "I'm guessing that they already know about this problem so I won't bother telling anyone."

Communication with your customers needs to be honest and invite feedback. Written customer satisfaction surveys are one way to get feedback, but they don't always provide an accurate picture. Most customers don't want to take time from their busy schedules to answer the questions and they're even less likely to write their opinions on the comment lines.

It's important to make it easy for your customers to give you timely, honest feedback. This means developing a system where complaints are invited and recognized as tools for developing stronger customer relationships.

Telephone and face-to-face conversations are the perfect time to invite customer comments. Here are a few tips:

- End each conversation with an open-ended question. For example: "What suggestions do you have on how we can provide even better service for you the next time you call?"

- Invite questions from your customers. For example: "Do you have any questions about the way we handle your service requests?"

- Be very gracious when a customer does complain. Always thank him or her for bringing the problem to your attention. Never get defensive.

No news is not usually good news when it comes to your customers. Inviting your customers to complain will make it easy for them to express their opinions. Complaints give your customers the opportunity to vent their frustrations so you can quickly resolve the problems before they decide to leave. They also generate ideas on how you can continually improve service delivery. But more importantly, encouraging ongoing feedback will help you to cultivate loyalty with the most important people in your company—your customers.

WHAT ARE YOUR CUSTOMERS WORTH?

When you lose a single customer, you lose a lifetime opportunity of profitability with that individual. Do you know the value of your customers?

To determine the average lifetime value of your customers, estimate how much they will spend with your business on a monthly or annual basis and multiply it by the number of years they could potentially use your products or services. For example, if an average grocery customer purchases $100 worth of grocery products per week, 52 weeks a year, for approximately 45 years—their average lifetime value will be $234,000.

Don't stop there. Next, factor in how much your customers could potentially increase their spending each year because they are thrilled with your product and service. There's more! Now start calculating the value of all of the new customers that your loyal customers will refer to your business.

Here are some examples of the average lifetime values of customers in a variety of industries:

Life insurance owner	$97,000
Automobile owner	$200,000
Grocery customer	$300,000
Medical patient	$1,000,000

Just a 5 percent increase in customer retention can increase profitability by as much as 100 percent. It costs five times more to get a new customer than it does to keep an existing one. It is important that all employees within your organization understand the lifetime value of their customers. Then they can focus on building relationships with the very people who keep them in business.

NO NEED TO TEACH
YOUR CUSTOMERS A LESSON

"The customer is always right."

That phrase has sold millions of books and been the topic of many a motivational speech. But ask anyone who deals with customers on a regular basis and they'll tell you it's wrong. Customers are not always right. They make mistakes. Some customers are dishonest. Some customers are chronic complainers and some are downright nasty. But no matter how unpleasant a customer is, it is not your job to prove they're wrong or teach them a lesson.

The good news is that about 97 percent of customers are decent, reasonable people who just want to be treated with respect and feel appreciated for their business. They will sometimes become upset because a mistake was made, but they will generally forgive the error and continue to do business with you if the problem is resolved.

So what to do about the 2 or 3 percent of customers who can ruin your day with a single phone call? First, you need to remember that it's difficult to keep all customers happy all of the time. Here are some tips for dealing with customers who treat you poorly, use abusive language, yell at you or just make you feel awful:

Let your angry customer vent for a while.

When he or she comes up for air, offer to help. If your customer uses abusive or vulgar language, simply let him or her know that you'd be happy to help but you're unable to do so under these conditions. Advise your customer that you will need to end the conversation. Before you hang up, encourage him or her to call back when they are calmer so you can help them to get the problem resolved.

Put emotional distance between you and your customer.

Your customer's anger is not about you. It's his or her problem so choose not to take it personally. Even nice customers can get angry when they feel a company has mistreated them. Do the best you can to let your customer know you care.

Don't try to teach your customer a lesson.

It really doesn't matter whose mistake it was. You are not in your job to serve as a judge and jury every time a customer messes up. You don't need to point out the error of their ways. Simply review the problem and work toward resolving it.

Treat even your angry customers with respect.

You don't have to agree with your customer's opinion. Most people just want to know that someone is willing to listen and actually cares about their concerns. They may be having a horrible day. Maybe they've been through a service nightmare with your company and they're simply fed up by the time you get the call. Perhaps they are experiencing a personal tragedy and just taking it out on you.

When all else fails, give up.

Some customers will simply not give you the opportunity to fix their problems. If the same customer has a track record of abusive language and angry calls, it may be better to say "goodbye" to their business. This message needs to be communicated to the customer by your manager or business owner.

Learn to let go.

Don't carry the baggage of one angry customer over to your other customers. They deserve to be treated with warmth and kindness. If a customer has upset you, get up and walk away for a few minutes. Get a drink of water, take some deep breaths and allow yourself to get neutral before you take that next call.

Regardless of a customer's personality or communication style, he or she is still a customer. Your customers may not always be right, but they are the reason we're in business. Most problems are the result of a lack of communication. Focus on helping the customer, not proving them wrong—even when they are. A kind word, a listening ear and respect will teach them a far greater lesson than pointing out the error of their ways.

IS THE CUSTOMER ALWAYS RIGHT?

We've all heard the story about the business owner who posted a sign that reads:

1. The customer is always right.
2. If the customer is wrong, see Point 1.

This mission statement is honorable and acts under the assumption that each customer is reasonable. But what happens when the customer is wrong?

I was returning from a business trip and waiting for my flight in the Cincinnati Airport. Thirty minutes before our scheduled departure, an airline attendant announced that the flight would be delayed for at least an hour due to weather problems in another state. The inevitable groans from waiting passengers turned to astonished stares as a businessman stormed up to the counter and proceeded to scream at the attendant.

He demanded a flight to his destination. The attendant apologized and patiently informed him that there were no other flights available until well after his scheduled flight was due to arrive. His loud tirade continued with, "I'm a frequent flyer. I want you to get me on another flight immediately or give me a voucher for a free ticket."

If this gentleman was indeed a frequent traveler, he should certainly understand that an airline is at the mercy of weather conditions. There was nothing this attendant could do to get him on another flight. But especially if he is a frequent flyer, it is important to acknowledge his frustration and give him something of value to keep him coming back. The attendant handled it beautifully. She quietly said, "I know you are anxious to get home after your exhausting trip. Let me arrange for you to relax in our VIP lounge where you can have complimentary beverages and Internet service."

A few minutes later, an airport cart driver picked up the passenger and whisked him off to the VIP lounge. The customer was smiling as though he were royalty.

Now, you may ask yourself, "Was that fair to the other customers?" No, not really. After all, this man received special attention while the rest of us were still sitting in the general boarding area, patiently awaiting the arrival of our plane. But only a few people seated next to the counter had overheard the conversation. Instead of frustration, the other passengers were relieved that peace and quiet had been restored. Most were commenting on how well the flight attendant had maintained a calm and friendly manner.

Many executives and employees believe that most customers lie or make ridiculous demands in order to rip off the company. The reality is that only 2 to 3 percent of customers fall into this category. Yet, many organizations implement policies as a means of protection from their dishonest customers. Unfortunately, their policies often punish the 97 to 98 percent of customers who have legitimate complaints and requests.

What is the best way to deal with a customer who acts childish and irrational? Well, you may not like my answer, but you must treat your customers as if they're always right. This is perhaps one of the biggest challenges for customer service professionals. It's very difficult for you to identify those customers who actually want to take advantage of your company. Customers who complain strongly usually feel cheated or victimized. They also feel that their situation is the most important one in the world.

Here are five steps for dealing with irrational customers:

1. Try to put yourself in your customers' shoes. Ask yourself, "If this were me, what would I want?"

2. Remain calm and exercise patience. Getting into an argument will only increase your stress and escalate your customers' anger.

3. Trust your customers, even if you don't agree with their point of view.

4. Give your customers something of value that will keep them coming back. The higher the perceived value, the more impact it will have.

   For example, I recently stayed at a Marriott Hotel. Due to a processing error at the front desk, I did not receive my Marriott Rewards points or credits for my stay. Two weeks later, I notified the general manager. He was out so his assistant made sure I received credit for my stay and added 5,000 bonus reward points as an apology for my inconvenience. What was the cost to the Marriott? Nothing. What did the hotel receive in return for its recovery efforts? I'm telling you about it and I've just booked a reservation at another Marriott.

5. Recognize that all customers are not equal. A long-time, valued customer who has spent large sums of money with your organization may require a higher level of compensation for service recovery than a brand new or intermittent customer.

Is the customer always right? No. But you must treat him or her as if he or she is.

DEFENSIVENESS DESTROYS CUSTOMER RELATIONSHIPS

Our family took a trip that was part of a group tour. When we arrived at our destination, one of the guests became extremely upset. It had taken nearly an hour for his family to be checked in at our hotel. This occurred after we had just completed an eight-hour plane ride followed by a five-hour bus trip.

While this same family was finally getting settled in their room, the tour bus departed without them. The entire group was on their way to attend a professional soccer game in Valencia. The tour guide never noticed that the family had been left behind. When we arrived at the stadium, several guests pointed out that this family was missing. The tour guide chose not to return to the hotel to retrieve them even though it was only 20 minutes away. He simply shrugged and stayed for the game.

Upon returning to the hotel, the guest angrily confronted the tour guide (who also happens to be the owner of the company). Rather than apologize and take ownership of his mistake, the owner became very defensive and the two had a heated argument. Many of the other guests witnessed the interaction and it set an underlying negative tone for the rest of the trip. Several impressions of the tour guide were formed during that single argument, none of them were flattering. Every time there was a miscommunication or a minor problem, it was underscored by the fact that many of the adults on the trip had decided they didn't like the tour guide.

When dealing with an angry customer, you have a variety of options on how you choose to respond. Among them are ignoring your customer, rolling your eyes, pretending you're listening while doing other things, actively listening, or defending yourself. Of these options, the one that can do the most damage is taking a defensive posture. The minute you start defending yourself or your company, you have created a lose-lose situation. Your customer will never agree with your side of the issue and all you will have accomplished is escalating their anger.

When you argue with a customer and try to prove your point, the customer may think that you are questioning their honesty or integrity. You are also telling your customer that he or she has no right to be angry. But, most importantly, you are clearly demonstrating to the customer that you are unwilling to take ownership of service.

Within two hours of the argument that took place in our hotel lobby, every adult on the trip was fully aware of what occurred. The guest had vented his frustrations with the tour guide by telling everyone who would listen. The negative word-of-mouth spread like wildfire. For the rest of the trip (remember, this was the first day), people were looking for problems with the tour guide. Several days into the trip, the wife of the angry guest tried to diplomatically give some feedback to the tour guide's wife. There were several of us sitting together at dinner when she suggested ways on how the situation could have been handled differently.

To our surprise, the tour guide's wife blurted out in anger, "We're the experts here and I don't want to hear any more about this."

Thankfully, we all had a wonderful time despite these problems, but her comment pretty much sealed the deal on whether or not anyone on the trip will ever travel with that tour company again. I'm certain that the negative word-of-mouth will continue to circulate throughout our community, as well.

The negative aftermath could have been easily avoided if the tour guide had taken responsibility for the problems that occurred.

DISSATISFIED CUSTOMERS ARE GOLD

To retain customers, a company needs to prove that it can provide good service on a regular basis, with mistakes being the exception rather than the standard operating procedure. Having to apologize too much is an indication that there are larger problems that need correcting.

In every business, mistakes happen and customers get angry. But when a problem is fixed properly and stays fixed ... customer loyalty actually increases!

If you are dealing with a customer who is angry, upset or concerned, following these five steps will not only resolve the problem, but may actually increase customer loyalty:

1.   **LISTEN** carefully to what your customer is telling you. Be sure that you are fully engaged in the conversation. You need to stop everything you are doing and give your customer 100 percent of your attention. Refrain from doing other tasks while the customer is talking. Active listening cannot be accomplished when you are distracted. Address each and every issue and concern raised by your customers. Don't ignore a complaint because you don't think it's important or you think the customer is wrong. Make no excuses while you are listening to a customer complaint. Hear your customers out and accept that their perception of the event is very real.

2.   **EMPATHIZE** with your customer's concerns. Let him or her know that you sincerely care about his problem even if you don't agree with his comments. No matter what your customer complains about, respond sincerely with these words, "Thank you for bringing this to my attention."

3.   **APOLOGIZE** even if it was not your fault. When expressed with sincerity, "I'm sorry" can go a long way toward calming down a customer. An apology implies that you are willing to take ownership of the problem. Apologizing to customers for mistakes is important and neces-

sary, but apologies are not free passes for providing bad service. Business leaders need to identify the times when their companies do deliver poor customer service and be able to correct problems when they occur. Apologizing is part of this recovery process.

4. **RESOLVE** the problem. Let customers know you are on their side and will do everything you can to help them get the problem resolved. If only an employee in another department can fix it, help to make the transition smooth so the customer doesn't have to repeat his or her request. Don't make amends by just providing the original product or service. Exceed your customers' expectations by offering them more. Starbucks has a policy that if a customer is dissatisfied with their coffee or has to wait too long, they get a certificate for a free drink on their next visit.

5. **NOW** is the time to address the problem. The faster a mistake is fixed, the more loyalty will actually increase. It is also more likely that the customer will give your company another chance.

Look at the first letters of each of the five steps: **L**isten, **E**mpathize, **A**pologize, **R**esolve and **N**ow. They spell **LEARN**. That's because every time a customer complains, it provides you with an opportunity to learn how you can do a better job and feel great about the positive difference you made in that person's day.

Customers are fragile. Let one drop and you break a profitable relationship. Great customer service starts with you. Don't preach it to others—live it. Do what it takes to get your customers to want to continue doing business with your company. Apologies are easy when you recognize their lasting value to your customer, your company and your job stability.

WHAT'S IRKING CONSUMERS?

A *Wall Street Journal* poll asked 1,034 consumers what irked them the most about service people. Here are some of their responses:

- ♦ Sales and delivery people who say they'll be at your home or office at a certain time but never show up (40 percent).
- ♦ Poorly informed salespeople (37 percent).
- ♦ Salesclerks who are on the phone while waiting on you (25 percent).
- ♦ Salesclerks who say, "It's not my department" (25 percent).
- ♦ Salespeople who talk down to you (21 percent).
- ♦ Salesclerks who can't describe how a product works (16 percent).

INVISIBLE EMPLOYEES MAKE CUSTOMERS DISAPPEAR

Stacie is a professional who works in a Milwaukee investment firm. After work one evening, she decided to take advantage of a big end-of-season sale at a local sporting goods store. As Stacie entered the store, she was greeted by an employee who informed her that ski jackets were located on the lower level. Soon, Stacie was engrossed in her search for the perfect jacket.

She had been shopping for over 30 minutes when she found what she wanted—a beautiful ski jacket that looked great on her and it was on sale. Around the same time as her discovery, it dawned on Stacie that she had been alone the whole time she had been shopping. Not one employee had approached her, talked to her or offered assistance. In fact, Stacie hadn't even seen an employee since she first stepped through the door. They knew she was there. After all, she was the only customer in the store. Adding to her frustration was the sound of employees chatting and laughing in the back room.

Since Stacie is a devoted "Loyalty Leader," she reluctantly placed her dream jacket back on the rack and marched out of the store. "It was a matter of principle," she said. "I hated to walk away from such a great deal, but I simply couldn't bring myself to purchase a product from people who obviously don't care about their customers."

Invisible employees are everywhere:

- The bank teller who tries not to make eye contact with the next person in line

- The waiter who stands in the corner of the restaurant gossiping with co-workers while customers are patiently awaiting refills on their coffee

- The service rep who reads her email messages while on the phone with a customer

- The postal worker who closes his window when there are 11 customers standing in line

- The boss who hides in her office and keeps her door closed

- The employee who sits in his cubicle listening to an iPod with headphones on while he's working

- The financial rep who doesn't stay in touch with her clients

- The contractor who doesn't come back to correct a problem with his remodeling job

Invisible employees will cause your customers to disappear. Poor time management, ineffective leadership, laziness, stress, high call volumes, apathy and boredom are just a few of the reasons employees become invisible.

In order for employees to take ownership of service, they need to participate in identifying ways to remove obstacles. Invite employees at all levels of the organization to help create guidelines that will make them become more visible to customers. Sample guidelines:

- Keep service windows open when there is more than one customer in line.

- Make eye contact with customers.

- Smile and greet every customer who comes within 10 feet of you.

- Set aside personal tasks such as reading email while interacting with a customer on the phone.

Don't give your customers reasons to disappear. Instead, focus on ways to create a warm, inviting environment for your customers.

NEGATIVE EMPLOYEES CAN POISON SERVICE

It isn't the people you fire who make your life
miserable; it's the people you don't.
~ Harvey Mackay

Do you find yourself dreading to come to work because of that particular employee who constantly complains? Do you need to do a "barometer check" on certain co-workers each morning to determine their mood of the day? Do you have a certain co-worker who always seems to get away with doing the minimum amount of effort each day while the other employees are working hard? Do you find yourself apologizing to customers because of the way a particular employee handled their service requests?

In their book, *How Full is Your Bucket?*, Tom Rath and Donald O. Clifton wrote:

> *It is possible for just one or two people to poison an entire workplace. And managers who have tried moving negative people to other departments to alleviate the problem know that 'location, location, location' doesn't apply to these people; they bring their negativity along with them wherever they go. Negative employees can tear through a workplace like a hurricane racing through a coastal town.*

A rude customer service representative greeted me when I called my airline to report that 2,800 miles I had earned on a recent trip had not been credited to my frequent flyer account. She said she could only give me the miles if I provided her with my ticket number. I explained that I no longer had my ticket because the flight attendant at the airport had assured me that the miles had been credited to my account.

Her reply? "That's your problem, not mine. You'll just have to call your travel agent and get the ticket numbers. Then you can call back and start over."

I called the travel agent to get the numbers. After much hassle, we tracked them down. The agent asked for the name of the rep I had dealt with at the airline. I said it was Kayla. First silence—then with a sigh, she said, "Ah yes, Kayla. We've complained about her a couple of times. I see it hasn't made a difference"

The next day I called the airline's frequent flyer customer service department. This time a warm, friendly employee, who proved to be extremely helpful, greeted me. I happened to mention the negative experience I had with the other rep. She apologized and asked if I knew the rep's name. I said it was Kayla.

First silence—then with a sigh, she said, "Ah yes, Kayla. She tends to rub our customers the wrong way. You're not the first person who's complained about her. Everyone else in our department is so nice and we really care about the customers but her attitude makes us all look bad."

An employee like Kayla is like a skunk in a field full of cats. She may look like the others but her negative attitude makes her service stink. Not only that, the behaviors of one employee can give customers the impression that the whole department and even the company stink.

Remember: "Sixty-eight percent of customers leave because of an attitude of indifference by a single employee."

When customers and co-workers have attached a negative attitude label to a specific employee, it's time to evaluate that employee's cost to the organization.

Negative employees cost a business money.

The cost of a negative employee can be measured in the following ways:

- The cost of losing an angry customer

- The cost of wasting time with re-work caused by the employee's refusal to handle the service properly the first time

- The cost of replacing employees who leave because they don't want to work with this negative employee

- The cost of negative word-of-mouth advertising (the travel agent tries not to work with this airline because of poor service experiences and complaints from her customers about the airline)

- The cost of overall diminished morale within the department

- The cost of time wasted by supervisor trying to fix the employee's attitude

Take a look at your field of great employees. Are skunks hiding there? How much damage are they doing to your co-worker and customer relationships? Is it worth it?

You may think you don't need customer service training because you do not directly deal with the external customers. Think again! Your customer is anyone who benefits from the work you do—or, conversely, suffers when your work is done poorly or not at all. Your work is part of a customer-supplier chain. It is not an isolated activity.

Customer loyalty starts within the organization. When you recognize that your co-workers are your primary customers, you can improve every employee's ability to deliver outstanding service to external customers.

GOOD INTENTIONS DON'T COUNT

While shopping one day I noticed a "No Wait" policy posted in a grocery store. The sign declared, "We guarantee that you will no longer experience long lines. When we see more than three people in line, we will open a new register immediately."

I had plenty of time to read the sign. There were six people in line ahead of me!

Customer service standards are only as good as the people who enforce them. Business leaders are filled with good intentions, but good intentions don't count. When it comes to the delivery of service, the only things that do count are the actions that customers actually experience.

If a company boasts about its customer service policies and then fails to deliver the promised service, it actually does more damage than if it had never created the standards in the first place. When this occurs, customer trust is replaced by skepticism.

When developing customer service standards for your organization, make sure they can realistically be supported through current staffing and budget. Customer service standards should be simple and easy to implement. Training should be provided at all levels of the organization so every employee knows the following:

♦   WHAT customer service actions are expected of them.

♦   HOW to deliver great customer service.

♦   WHEN to make exceptions in order to make the customer happy.

♦   WHY their role in customer service is important to their career and the success of the organization.

A recognition program needs to be in place in order to reward employees for delivering great customer service.

Accountabilities need to be defined so employees know how their customer service behavior will be measured. They also need to clearly understand the consequences when they fail to meet the service standards.

Great customer service intentions don't count unless they're backed up by actions and attitudes that demonstrate that you sincerely care about your customers. You can have real empathy for a customer, but if you are unable to communicate that empathy, your customer won't believe you're being sincere.

"Fine" is a Dangerous Word

Have you ever had a terrible customer service experience at a restaurant? When you were leaving, did the host or hostess ask, "How was everything?"

Instead of offering your real opinion, did you simply answer, "Fine?"

Most of us leave it at "fine" for a number of reasons. We don't want to waste our time trying to fix their business; we don't believe anyone will listen to our concerns; and even if they do listen, we don't believe anything will change. So we say "fine" and walk out the door vowing never to return. Then, on Monday morning, we go to work and tell everyone how awful our experience was at that restaurant.

"FINE" is the most dangerous word in the consumer language. It's a code word that means, "I'm neutral and as soon as I find something better, I'm out of here!"

Are your customers telling you that everything is fine, implying they are satisfied? If so, you may have a problem, because 65 to 85 percent of customers who say they are satisfied actually switch to the competition.

Customers will not continue to do business with you for long if you simply meet their expectations. In order to build loyalty, you must exceed expectations by looking for ways to surprise and delight your customers.

Don't settle for your customers checking the "satisfied" box on your satisfaction surveys. Build loyalty by providing exceptional service. Then, your loyal customers will be writing on your survey comment lines:

"The employees here are always friendly."
"This company goes the extra mile for me."
"The employees sincerely care about my concerns."

Satisfied customers are neutral and may be keeping one eye open for better options with your competitors. Strive for turning your satisfied customers into loyal customers.

SELF-ASSESSMENT

IS A CUSTOMER SERVICE JOB RIGHT FOR YOU?

Only competent, qualified people can deliver great customer service. Customer service skills can be learned, but employees need the right type of personality and attitude to support those skills. Before applying to any job that involves considerable customer interaction, take this short quiz as a self-assessment to help you determine whether or not customer service is right for you.

1. I know that my customers are the reason for my work, not an interruption of my tasks.
    True   False

2. I maintain a warm, friendly attitude toward my external and internal customers, no matter how busy I am.
    True   False

3. I take ownership of meeting customer needs and resolving customer complaints.
    True   False

4. I actively seek ways to make my customers and co-workers feel valued.
    True   False

5. I actively model the highest ethical and business standards for the company.
    True   False

6. I recognize that my co-workers are my customers and work toward building trust across departmental boundaries.
    True   False

7. I do not get defensive when I'm dealing with an angry customer.
    True   False

8. I exhibit patience, courtesy and respect to people, regardless of
    their behavior toward me.
    True   False

9. I offer solutions to customers rather than telling them what to do.
    True   False

10. I am committed to being a life-long learner by actively participating
    in training that can help me improve my skills.
    True   False

If you answered "True" to all of the questions, CONGRATULATIONS! A
customer service job is a good fit for you. The way you interact with
your customers can significantly impact the success of a company.

If you answered "False" to any of the questions, a customer service
position might not be the best fit for you.

It takes a person with a positive attitude, commitment to excellence,
and solid communication skills to build strong customer relationships.

CHAPTER 4

STEPS FOR BUILDING CUSTOMER LOYALTY

Customers don't care what you know, until they know that you care.
> — Digital Equipment Corporation,
> Customer Service Department

Do what you do so well that they will want to see it again and bring their friends.
> — Walt Disney

OLD-FASHIONED SERVICE STILL COUNTS

The Walgreen's chain was founded in Chicago, Illinois in 1901. It started out as a drug store with a fanatically customer-oriented owner, Charles R. Walgreen, Sr.

There is a notable and often told story of how Mr. Walgreen would deliver the drugs to his customers in the early days of Walgreen's. A customer would call the pharmacy and place an order for medication. Mr. Walgreen would repeat back the order loud enough so that his assistant could hear it. The assistant would then fill the prescription and deliver the order to the customer's home while Mr. Walgreen continued the phone conversation.

Often times, the customer would need to interrupt his phone conversation with Mr. Walgreen, saying, "Oh, someone's at the door. Could you excuse me for a moment?" When he answered the door, he was surprised by the assistant, who handed him the prescription he had ordered just minutes earlier. Customers started telling their family, friends and neighbors about this amazing service. Word-of-mouth spread quickly and Walgreens expanded throughout the United States.

The type of service outlined in the Walgreen's story seems old-fashioned in this day and age. High volumes of orders, lack of time, cost and staffing limitations all present barriers. But even with these challenges, it is still possible to deliver amazing customer service. As a matter of fact, it's easier than ever to exceed customer expectations. In most instances, time-starved customers don't expect your undivided attention. They simply want good, old fashioned service that is delivered by a friendly person.

It doesn't matter how great a company's customer service philosophy looks on paper, exceptional customer service is only as good as the employees who are interacting with the customers. It's really quite simple. Just follow these old fashioned principles:

- ♦   Extend old-fashioned courtesies. Say "please" and "thank you" to your customers.

- ♦   Wear an old-fashioned smile, even when you're on the phone. Warm up the conversation by taking a few extra minutes to chat with your customers.

- ♦   Treat your customers with old-fashioned respect. Honor their busy schedules by removing service obstacles that waste their time, such as voice mail systems that are difficult to navigate.

- Wear clothing that reflects good taste and send a message of old-fashioned professionalism.

- Demonstrate old-fashioned patience when listening to your customer's concerns.

Remember that without these customers, you wouldn't have a good, old-fashioned job!

LOYALTY IS BUILT
ONE CUSTOMER AT A TIME

In most industries, when customers get angry, they punish the company by taking their business elsewhere. Customer frustrations increase when they receive poor service from a company that is the only game in town. Historically, companies that have a monopoly on service have been accused of taking their customers for granted.

Not so at Rochester Public Utilities (RPU) in Rochester, Minnesota. The employees of RPU recognize that, for the most part, their customers are stuck with them. They rely on RPU for electric and water service. There are no other utility company options available.

The employees of this company believe that because their customers don't have the option to take their business elsewhere, they owe it to them to deliver the best service possible. RPU serves over 42,000 electric customers and over 31,000 water customers, but the employees are committed to delivering outstanding service, one customer at a time.

Take, for example, Jim Himango. Jim has been with RPU for 37 years. His title is Heavy Crew Foreman in construction, maintenance and field operations. In essence, Jim oversees the work of the linemen responsible for electric transmission and distribution. It could become very easy for a seasoned veteran like Jim to get comfortable and develop apathy toward his customers. Instead, he consistently demonstrates the importance of delivering caring service.

In one instance, Jim and his crew were involved in a six-week project. Each day, while he was at the customer's site, he noticed a 9-year-old boy watching the guys work. He took time to get to know the boy, explained to him what the crew was working on and even allowed him to hand tools to the linemen. One day, under the parents' supervision, Jim showed the boy the bucket truck and let him climb in.

When the job was completed, Jim went the extra mile. He invited this boy and his parents to visit the company's headquarters. They received a tour of the facility and at the end of the tour, he presented his little friend with a brand-new, toy bucket truck. The boy's parents were delighted.

Jim recognized that customer loyalty is built one customer at a time. The crews who are on-site at their customers' homes and businesses sometimes have much greater impact on those customer relationships than the customer service representatives.

IT'S CALLED SERVICE FOR A REASON

Organizations have more to fear from lack of quality internal customer service than from any level of external customer service.

—Ron Tillotson

Service is a simple concept that involves every employee in the organization. Good service is only as good as your customers believe it to be. Customer perception is all that really matters. No matter how wonderful the company's customer service motto sounds, in the end, the ultimate reality is how the customers feel about the way they were treated. When customers feel they've been treated well, they'll be happy and continue to do business with the organization. If customers feel they've been treated poorly, they'll be unhappy, and tell everyone they know.

Everyone in your organization is part of a customer service chain. No matter what your role, you are providing service for other people. They may be internal customers, such as employees in your department or employees working in a different division of the organization. The employees you serve may also serve only internal customers. But eventually, the chain will reach the external customers.

Delivering a high level of customer satisfaction relates to everything that anyone in the organization does. Customer service is everyone's responsibility. It doesn't matter whether you work in information technology, purchasing, legal, accounting, human resources, the warehouse, executive operations or any other area-- you are a customer service professional.

An organization-wide customer service approach is important because your customers perceive the company as a whole. When problems occur, your customers do not say, "Well, a staff member in the public relations department messed up." They say, "The XYZ Company messed up!"

Instead of pigeonholing customer service into a single department, it is far more effective for every employee in every department to do his or her part in the customer service effort. In fact, maybe every department should be called Customer Service.

No matter what your industry, no matter what your job title, you work for the customer. No customer calls or walks in your door and says, "What can I do for the XYZ Company today?" They are asking, "What can XYZ do for me today?"

Customers can tell when the whole organization is service-oriented. Customer service no longer means how fast you answer the phone. It means quality products, on-time delivery, responsiveness to complaints, after-sale support, accurate billing, clear communications and everything else. These goals can only be achieved with a total service commitment by every employee on the customer service chain.

After all, they call it "service" for a reason.

CAT-ASTROPHIC SERVICE

Sometimes things go wrong even when we're trying to provide great customer service. Check out this true story shared by the big, burly contractor we hired to remodel our bathroom.

He was working at another house when the owner announced she had to run some errands. She told him he could continue working while she was gone as long as he kept an eye on her cat. It seems Fluffy had a habit of sneaking out.

Wanting to prove he was trustworthy, the contractor carefully slipped out the door each time he went to his truck for tools and supplies. When he returned, he always made sure Fluffy was safely in the house.

After working a few hours in the tight confines of the bathroom, he got warm. So he decided to open the window just a few inches to let in some fresh air. A couple of hours later, he stopped to take a break and looked out the window.

There was Fluffy, staring back at him from outside. Panic-stricken, he opened the window and tried to coax Fluffy back in. She wouldn't budge. He located her favorite toys and jiggled them in front of her, all the time calling, "Here kitty, kitty." No luck. So he ran downstairs to the kitchen and frantically searched the cupboards for kitty treats.

He found them and raced back upstairs to find the cat still sitting outside. He laid a trail of treats along the window sill calling, "Come and get your treat, Fluffy."

Finally, much to his relief, the cat stepped back in. He quickly shut the window and breathed a huge sigh of relief.

When the owner returned he decided not to tell her what had happened because he didn't want to upset her.

Now that's a great example of going the extra mile for a customer, but unfortunately it's not the end of the story.

The following day he showed up to complete the job. The owner greeted him at the front door and she was furious! It turns out he let the wrong cat into her home. While he was coaxing the stray cat in, Fluffy had been in the house the whole time hiding in a bedroom.

The two cats had discovered one another around 2:00 a.m. and a huge cat fight ensued with much howling and hissing. It took Fluffy's owner over an hour to get the strange cat out of the house!

Loyalty is Built Through C.A.R.I.N.G. Service

Voice mail, automated phone systems, email and other technology have replaced the personal touch when it comes to customer service. Customer frustrations are on the rise. Their number-one complaint is that no one really seems to care anymore.

Your customer can tell the difference between satisfactory service and caring service. Satisfactory service is what most customers expect. This type of service focuses on completing a task rather than building a relationship with the customer.

Satisfactory implies adequate, good enough and acceptable. Customers who are merely satisfied with your business can be wooed away by others who offer something better.

Customers are discouraged by poor service and expectations are low. The simple gesture of showing your customers that you care about them will be a welcome surprise compared to the apathy they experience elsewhere.

Building customer loyalty boils down to one simple concept: C.A.R.I.N.G.

C = Consistent

Customer loyalty is earned. Commit to delivering exceptional customer service with every customer interaction, every day.

- ◆ Show your customers you value their business by taking complete ownership of their concerns and happiness.
- ◆ Provide each of your customers with respect, friendliness and knowledge, whether you communicate face-to-face, by telephone or through email.
- ◆ Maintain a positive attitude—all the time!
- ◆ Deliver consistent quality and sign your work with excellence.

A = Attentive

Your customer is not an interruption of your work. He or she is the reason you're at work.

- ◆ Take time to listen carefully to your customers. Don't rush through service.
- ◆ Focus on what your customer needs and avoid distractions so you can give your customer 100 percent of your attention.
- ◆ Your customer took the time to do business with you. Honor that decision by taking the time to deliver a quality experience.

R = Reliable

When you make a promise to a customer—keep it. Take responsibility for meeting your customers' needs.

- Project a professional image through the way you dress. Don't wear clothing that can offend or embarrass your customers. Dress in a manner that enhances your credibility and positively reflects on the organization.

- Maintain order in your workspace.

- Be completely honest with your customers.

- Communicate with a warm, friendly tone of voice.

- Avoid the use of jargon or slang. Be careful not to talk "down" to your customers or co-workers.

- Build your reputation of reliability through clear communications, accuracy and consistent follow-through.

- Focus on timeliness. Respond quickly to your customers' and co-workers' requests. Show up for work and meetings on time. Return phone calls promptly and deliver information on time.

- Promptly reply to email messages.

- Commit to professional development by attending workshops and seminars, and reading materials that will help you to learn and grow in your ability to do your job better.

I = Individualized

No two customers are alike. Each customer has individual needs and concerns. Pay attention to your customer's tone of voice and actions.

Recognize that your customers have unique styles. A dominant customer may seem impatient and will want to control the situation to get his desired results. A shy customer may need assurance and guarantees. An outgoing customer may require more "chat" time. You can build rapport quickly by learning to respond appropriately with each type of customer.

- Learn your customers' names and ask about their families.

- Congratulate your customers when you learn of their celebrations, such as a birthday, arrival of a new baby or purchase of a new home.

- Ask your customers for advice on how you or your company could better serve them. Encourage their feedback and ideas, and yes, even criticism. Then listen.

- Sincerely compliment your customers every chance you get. Compliment them on how nicely they're dressed, their pleasant phone voice, or their patience during a long wait. Don't mistake compliments with false flattery.

- Surprise your customers by delivering unexpected service, such as free shipping or a little something extra to show them they're appreciated.

- Keep your customers informed about the status of their order, any delays or obstacles to meeting their needs and changes in policies that may affect them.

N = Notable

Is your service worth bragging about? Word-of-mouth is the most powerful marketing campaign of all. Give your customers quality service that they can brag about.

- Greet each customer as you would a friend—someone you are glad to speak with.

- When you hear repeated complaints about something, take the initiative to fix the problem! For example, if more than one customer complains that the music is too loud when they are on "hold," take the initiative to have the volume turned down.

- A warm, friendly response to a complaint will exceed most customers' expectations.

- Notice their needs. If customers sound rushed or stressed, acknowledge their busy schedules and do everything you can to speed up their service experience.

- Look for ways to remove service obstacles that may waste your customers' time. This can be as simple as making sure there is a working pen on the counter if they need to sign a form or credit card receipt.

- If you need to transfer a customer call, stay on the line to explain the situation to your co-worker so your customer doesn't need to repeat his or her request. Offer to call the customer after you have resolved his or her complaints so the customer doesn't need to remain on the line while you track down the cause of the problem.

- Stand by your promises. Return calls at precisely the time you said you would call. Don't put a customer in a position of having to call back to remind you that they are still waiting for information.

- Never promise service by a co-worker unless you are certain that he or she will be able to deliver on that promise for the customer.

G = Generous

Be generous with your service and look for opportunities to go the extra mile for your customers.

- Whenever possible, bend a rule or make an exception when your customer has a special need.

- Deliver more than expected. This may mean chatting a little longer with a customer who sounds lonely or just wants to visit. You can waive a shipping charge if an order has been delayed.

- ◆ Congratulate your customers on their achievements— when they've been appointed to a board, received a promotion or landed that important client.

- ◆ Surprise and delight your customers with unexpected service such as a follow-up phone call or handwritten "thank you" note.

- ◆ Reward your loyal customers with a surprise "thank you" gift—a box of chocolates, gift card, calendar, etc. Be sure to write a note to let your customers know that this is a gift of appreciation just for doing business with you.

- ◆ When your customers make appointments to meet with you, take them early.

- ◆ Introduce your customers to other members of the team, especially staff who only deal with internal customers.

- ◆ Slip your customers a handwritten "thank-you" note when they've been patient, when they've complained, when they've referred a new customer or just to thank them for being a loyal customer.

- ◆ Hold monthly contests for your customers where they can win prizes.

- ◆ Actively seek out and participate in community outreach and service events or causes that your customers care about.

- ◆ Give each of your best customers a standing ovation the next time they walk through the door.

- ◆ Create over-satisfied customers by frequently asking your customers, "How can we do an even better job of serving your needs?"

Put value on what's important to your customers, not what's important to you. People are loyal to a business when they feel they've been treated well and received good value for their money. Customer service goes a long way toward pleasing customers on both counts.

C.A.R.I.N.G. customer service means going out of your way for customers, doing everything possible to meet their needs and sometimes making decisions that benefit customers, even at a minor expense to the company.

FIVE KEYS TO CUSTOMER LOYALTY

Family

- ◆ Use your customer's name at least three times in every conversation.

- ◆ Remember personal details such as birthdays, children's names and accomplishments.

Friendly

- ◆ Smile every time you are on the telephone.

- ◆ Demonstrate enthusiasm and joy when helping your customers.

Flexible

- ◆ Think of yourself as your customer's partner.

- ◆ Look for ways to bend the rules and remove service obstacles.

Follow-up

- ◆ A follow-up phone call or handwritten note is a powerful loyalty-building tool.

- ◆ You can never thank your customers or co-workers too often.

- ◆ Keep your promises.

Fast

◆ Time is everyone's most precious commodity. Respect your customer's time and schedule.

◆ On the one hand, your customers want fast service. On the other hand, once they have your attention, they want you to take time with them.

TAKE A FIELD TRIP TO IMPROVE CUSTOMER SERVICE

Do you wish your co-workers would take ownership of service? Do you want to identify all the customer loyalty barriers in your company? Do you want lots of creative solutions for removing those barriers? Do you want to build employee loyalty?

If you answered "Yes" to any of these questions, try out this idea that I've used to help several of my clients identify and re-solve many of their customer service issues: organize teams of up to ten employees and schedule quarterly field trips through your company.

If possible, try to have members of different departments rep-resented on each team. What? You're the ONLY employee? It doesn't matter. Just schedule your own private field trip through your business.

Here's your first field trip theme: "Customer Loyalty Barriers."

Give each member of the field trip team a worksheet where he or she can write down every customer service barrier they see. Encourage them to be creative and look beyond the obvious barri-ers. You can have some fun and tell everyone to dress for a safari and hand out binoculars. Remember, though, that the objective is very serious. Here are some trouble spots to watch for:

- Signs that look unprofessional (handwritten), have confusing messages or give orders to your customers
- Employees who are dressed too casually or appear unkempt
- Long lines
- Inadequate phone system or long wait times for phone service
- Business hours that are inconvenient for your target market
- Gossiping employees (particularly when they are visible to your customers)
- Unclean restrooms or drinking fountains
- Litter on the floor or overflowing wastebaskets, both inside and outside the building
- UNSMILING EMPLOYEES
- Poor lighting
- Outdated magazines in the waiting room
- Unsafe or inconvenient parking

In a nutshell, if you're placing service obstacles in the path of your customers, you're losing customers. When you remove obstacles, customer loyalty goes up. It's that simple.

Here are some more field trip themes:

- Customer loyalty builders. What are you and your coworkers doing well?
- Opportunities to go the extra mile
- Ways to make customers feel welcome
- Ways to thank your customers
- Ways to make customers feel valued

SOMETIMES KNOWLEDGE TRUMPS KINDNESS

When I checked in at my airline's desk in Milwaukee, the young lady behind the counter informed me that my flight was delayed by two hours. She was very friendly and said with a smile, "I sure don't want you to miss your connecting flight to Sacramento so let me help you get on the express bus to O'Hare. We need to hurry, it's leaving in a few minutes."

She quickly issued me a boarding pass for the plane I would board in Chicago. Then she grabbed my suitcase and said, "Come on. I'll help you get your luggage to the bus. She ran ahead and told the bus driver to wait.

I wasn't happy about riding the bus for 90 minutes, especially when I found out that I had to pay the driver $25 in order to do so. But it was comfortable and it was important that I made it on time so I settled into my seat. The nice lady from United Airlines waved goodbye and wished me a safe trip. She sure was pleasant.

After my meeting the next day, I was in the Sacramento Airport trying to check in, but the system wouldn't acknowledge my reservation. I asked the clerk to help me. She rolled her eyes and reluctantly came around the counter to help me access the system. After three tries, I said, "Do you think you could just look up my reservation?"

She replied, "Management wants us to encourage the passengers to use the self-serve terminals."

"But it isn't working, and when I checked in at the airport in Milwaukee, a very nice clerk took care of it for me, plus she helped me to catch a bus since my flight was delayed."

"Well, the clerk may have been nice, but she didn't do her job correctly. She didn't cancel that part of your ticket so you were listed as a 'no show' for your flight. As a result, the rest of your ticket has been cancelled. Plus, according to our records, the flight was only delayed by nine minutes not two hours. You did not need to take the bus all the way to Chicago."

As you can imagine, the more she shared, the more frustrated I became. She didn't exude friendliness and she never smiled once, but she did say, "I'll be able to get this corrected so you can get on your return flight, but it's nearly full so you won't have the same seat assignment."

When she handed me my boarding pass, I was relieved and I thanked her. As I walked to the gate, I asked myself, "In a situation like this, would I rather have kindness or knowledge?" The honest answer? Knowledge.

Friendly service does not help the customer if it isn't backed up by sufficient knowledge to get the job done right. The warm, friendly clerk who made me feel so loved in Milwaukee actually caused me considerable inconvenience and worry.

Customers deserve to be treated with kindness, but their time is extremely valuable. When you do a job for a customer, review your work to be sure the job is done right the first time. If you're unsure, check with a trusted colleague before you send the customer on his or her way. Kindness doesn't count if the tasks are done wrong. It only ends up wasting time and frustrating the customer to the point that they will choose to take their business elsewhere. I know I will.

WALK IN YOUR CUSTOMERS' SHOES

Sometimes we become so focused on all the tasks that need to get done at work that we lose sight of our customers' perceptions.

The start of the new year is a perfect time to take a trip through your company while walking in your customers' shoes. In order to be a loyalty leader, you need to have a clear understanding of how your customers feel whenever they do business with you.

You can start by calling yourself at work. Call in to your direct line and listen carefully to your voice mail recording. What kind of message does it convey? Are you hearing a warm, friendly person on the phone who sincerely sounds like they want to help?

Next, pretend you're a customer who is about to make a service request that you typically handle. Without identifying who you are, call the company and request service. Pay attention to details such as how difficult or easy it is to navigate through the company's voice mail system. Note how long you need to wait before you actually speak with a live human being.

When you are actually speaking with an employee, ask questions that are often asked by customers. Is the information communicated clearly and respectfully?

Ask to have your call transferred to another department that deals with external customer requests. Evaluate how the transfer was handled. Did the employee take ownership of the call? Did they offer to contact someone directly in the other department? Did he or she give you a name and number just in case the call was dropped?

If you work in a retail environment, make a visit to the store on your day off and get a feel for what it's like to be treated as a customer. If your co-workers can identify you, ask a friend or family member to shop in the store and give you feedback on the customer service experience. You can observe from a distance. This is not like being a secret shopper where employees are being measured on their customer service performance. It is simply an exercise in perception so you can gain insight into your customers' experience.

The greater your understanding of how your customers feel when they do business with you, the greater your empathy will be for their needs and requests. Walk in your customers' shoes a few times and then evaluate what you could do differently to make their experience more positive. It is usually just the little things that need tweaking such as remembering to smile when you're speaking on the phone. Or, using words like "please," "thank you" and "I'm sorry" during customer conversations.

With every customer interaction you have, ask yourself, "If this were me, what would I want?" When you pause to think about this, it may change what you decide to do next.

The Four Cornerstones
of Great Service

Delivering value-added service is only one way to exceed your customers' expectations. You can set high standards when providing all aspects of customer service.

Give focus to your customer service efforts by establishing four cornerstones to target your goals:

1. **Welcoming Customers:**

   ♦ Welcome every customer who walks through the door or calls your company.

   ♦ Follow the 10-10 Rule (Greet customers within 10 seconds of coming within 10 feet of them).

   ♦ Smile and make eye contact.

   ♦ Make sure all voice mail messages are warm, friendly and welcoming.

◆ Invite your customers back every time they do business with you.

2. Valuing Customers:

◆ Remove service obstacles whenever possible.

◆ Tell them how they can take advantage of special offers.

◆ Let them know how long their service request may take.

◆ Use customers' names if known. If they are regular customers, ask for their names.

◆ Patiently answer all their questions.

◆ Take time with each customer. Don't rush service or let your tone of voice imply that you're too busy to help.

3. Thanking Customers:

◆ Thank the customer first when he or she expresses a complaint and take action to get it resolved.

◆ Thank a customer for trying out a new service or product.

◆ Thank a customer for their patience if they had to wait.

4. Going the Extra Mile for Customers:

◆ Offer to follow up with additional information.

◆ Point out other services you've provided at no additional cost.

◆ Ask how their experience was and if they have suggestions for improvements.

- Refer them to the competition if your company does not offer what they need.

- Listen carefully to their needs and offer creative solutions.

Your Customer's Bill of Rights

In 2007, David Neelman, CEO of JetBlue Airways, presented a new Customer Bill of Rights in response to the flood of complaints the company was receiving. Winter storms caused flight cancellations, delays and myriad other problems for JetBlue staff and customers. Neelman admitted that the company did a poor job of handling the problems. He issued a personal promise that JetBlue management has learned from its mistakes and pointed out that significant changes were taking place to support the company's commitment to excellent customer service.

In his message, Neelman took ownership of the problems that occurred and asked his customers to give JetBlue another chance. The Bill of Rights outlined specific actions that JetBlue will take when customers are inconvenienced due to overbooking, departure delays and ground delays. Many of the actions include compensating customers for being inconvenienced. For example, under the heading of Overbooking, it states that, "Customers who are involuntarily denied boarding shall receive $1,000."

I give David Neelman a great deal of credit for publicly admitting the mistakes that were made, taking ownership of the problems and very quickly introducing the solutions. He held himself accountable for his promise of improvement by posting the Customer's Bill of Rights on the company website.

Customers want more service today than they did 20 years ago when the trend was "self-serve." In a survey from the Marketing Science Institute of Cambridge, researchers found these factors were the most important characteristics of quality service:

- ◆ **Reliability**: Customers want companies to deliver dependable, accurate and consistent service.

- ◆ **Responsiveness**: Companies should be helpful and provide prompt service.

- ◆ **Assurance**: Employees should be knowledgeable, courteous and convey confidence in their ability to deliver great service.

- ◆ **Tangibles**: Facilities and equipment should be attractive and clean, and employees should be well groomed.

- ◆ **Empathy**: Customers want to receive individualized attention by employees who listen to them.

Before you develop a specific Bill of Rights for your company, recognize that it's up to you to provide basic rights with every customer interaction.

Your customers have the right to expect the following from you:

- ◆ A well-groomed, professional image
- ◆ Your undivided attention while they are speaking to you
- ◆ Prompt service that doesn't feel rushed
- ◆ A warm, friendly, positive attitude
- ◆ Appreciation from you for their business
- ◆ An open, receptive response to their feedback or complaints
- ◆ Knowledge about your products and/or services
- ◆ Honesty and integrity
- ◆ Fair prices
- ◆ A team approach to service

Many elements in a customer's Bill of Rights will be basically the same, regardless of the industry or organization. But it's important to recognize that your customers may differ from everybody else's customers in discernable ways. It boils down to truly understanding what your customers want and need. The best way to find out is to ask the employees who serve them.

Once you know your customers' needs and wants, you can translate them into specific actions and procedures that will build customer loyalty. This will enable you to go beyond the basics to exceed your customers' expectations.

LITTLE THINGS MATTER TO YOUR CUSTOMERS

My husband, Larry, told me that, 30 years ago, when he was deciding which university to attend, he had narrowed it down to two schools. Both universities had beautiful campuses and outstanding reputations. I asked, "What made you choose Purdue over the other school?"

"The doors were open at Purdue," he replied.

Intrigued, I wanted to know more. He explained that he had visited both universities without scheduling appointments. He wanted to tour the campuses and informally meet with members of the faculty who would be his professors.

At each school, Larry visited the department where the majority of his course work would take place. He walked down the corridor at the first school. Every faculty member had his or her office door closed. In order for him to speak with the professors, Larry had to knock and wait to be invited in to chat.

When he visited Purdue, he walked through the department and noticed that every office door was open. The professors looked up as he walked by, waved and invited him in for a chat. Larry chose Purdue.

He said, "I know it sounds like a little thing, but it made all the difference. I just got the feeling that the professors would be more caring and friendly."

Universities are big businesses. They all try to recruit great students with slick marketing materials and advertising campaigns. But just like other businesses, in the end, it's the little things that matter most. Students and parents are a university's primary customers. Many of these customers choose their schools based on how they "feel" about the people who work there.

In all businesses, it's the little things that count toward building customer loyalty. I'm a frequent visitor to a local coffee shop. I enjoyed going there because the manager knew my name and always greeted his customers with a smile. His attitude was contagious with the employees and it just plain "felt good" to go there.

Two months ago, he was transferred to a different store. The mood has changed dramatically. The new manager frequently "hides" in the back room. She rarely smiles and I've never heard her ask or mention a customer's name. One of the employees told me, "Several of our customers have called the corporate office to request the old manager. We've even lost some of our regulars because they say it's no fun to come in here anymore."

Here are 10 "little" things you can do right away to build customer loyalty:

1. Greet your customers with a smile (even on the telephone).

2. Thank your customers often and sincerely.

3. Prevent your customers from waiting too long— apologize if they do wait.

4. Be willing to say "I'm sorry" when something has gone wrong.

5. Learn your customers' names. Use them.

6. Maintain a professional image at all times.

7. Don't chew gum in front of your customers.

8. Listen patiently when your customer needs to complain.

9. Never complain about work or a co-worker where a customer might hear you.

10. Treat your co-workers with kindness and respect. Your customers are watching!

Customer expectations are not complicated. Your customers notice and appreciate the "little things" that will either lead them to loyalty or out the door—to the competition.

GIVE YOUR CUSTOMERS SOLUTIONS INSTEAD OF EXCUSES

While waiting to pay for my muffin and juice at a Minneapolis airport restaurant, a gentleman asked the cashier if he could get change when she opened the register.

"Absolutely not," she replied. "I'm way too busy to be giving out change."

"Please?" the man asked.

"No," she said. "Just look around you. Can't you see we're short-staffed?"

The cashier could have easily made change in less time than it took her to make excuses for denying this simple service request. Instead, she lost a potential customer and left a bad impression on everyone who was standing in line.

The cashier could have completely changed the situation by saying, "I'd be happy to, sir. Can you give me a few minutes while I take care of these customers first?" It's that simple. No matter what industry you're in, your customers want you to focus on outcomes, not obstacles.

There are times when it is difficult to deliver great customer service. Organizational barriers such as short staffing, computer problems, vendor delays, phone system problems and other issues will get in your way. Customers understand that these things can happen, but they don't want to hear them used as excuses for poor service. Instead, they want to know how and when the problem will be resolved. If they have been inconvenienced, they want to know what you will do to make it up to them.

On a trip to present training to a sales team for a company in South Dakota, my flight was delayed three times. I was going to be late for the scheduled workshop. I called my client every time I received a schedule update so he could make adjustments on his end and communicate the changes to his team. I didn't just show up late and then make excuses that the airlines messed up. I kept him posted and offered him the option of running the workshop a little later. Because I knew his team had already put in a long day, I tightened up some of my material in order to get them out at a reasonable time for dinner.

Use "solution-oriented" language when communicating with your customers, such as:

◆ **"How can I help?"**
Customers want the opportunity to explain in detail what they want. Don't try to guess what they need or offer a solution until they've had an opportunity to tell you.

◆ **"I'd be happy to solve that problem."**
Most customers, especially business-to-business customers, are looking to buy solutions. They want to know you are on their side and that you are positioning yourself as a partner in their success.

- **"Great question; let me find out."**
  When you don't know the answer, admit it, or you can hurt your credibility. But quickly follow up with a response that lets your customer know you are not giving him or her the brush-off. They want to know that you will help them find the correct answer.

- **"I will take ownership of your request."**
  Tell your customer you realize it's your responsibility to assist them in their service request. Reassure your customer by confirming that you fully understand what they need.

- **"I will keep you posted."**
  Customers trust vendors who keep them apprised of the status of their orders. Whether the news is good or bad, stay in touch with your customers to give them updates.

- **"I will keep my promises."**
  Whether it's a due date, a follow-up phone call or another promise, make sure your customer can count on you to deliver at the promised day and time.

- **"It'll be just what you ordered."**
  If the customer is not completely satisfied, do whatever it takes to correct the problem.

- **"I appreciate the opportunity to work with you."**
  Demonstrate your sincere appreciation through follow-up calls, hand-written thank-you notes and invitations to your customers to give you honest feedback on their service experience.

===

WHEN THE CABLE GUYS CAME CALLING

TV repairmen are often ridiculed for their lack of customer service skills. Unfortunately, this type of ridicule can be based on poor service delivered by just a few employees, but the damage translates to the image of the whole company.
Here's an example of exceptional customer service and the difference the efforts of only two employees can make to a company.

My Christmas gift to our family one year was a large, flat -screen TV. My husband, Larry, loves sports. So does my son. So when they asked me if we could also get cable TV in-stalled, I reluctantly said, "Yes."

Of course, I was the only one at home the day the cable man arrived. He wasn't a direct employee of Time Warner cable. Instead, he worked for a firm with which the company contracts installation services. The installer was pleasant enough. He inspected our outside wire and quickly got every-thing inside hooked up. Our new TV hadn't yet been deliv-ered, so he prepared the cable and showed me how to attach it. He was done with everything in 30 minutes.

Four days later, our new HDTV arrived and things weren't working properly. I promptly called Time Warner Cable and they scheduled another visit. This time, two young men who are direct employees of Time Warner showed up right on schedule. I immediately noticed a huge difference in their attitudes compared with the first guy. I was delighted the moment Aaron Stephens and his apprentice, Randee Drew, walked through the door. They greeted us with big smiles and said, "Let's get things working for you." It was wet outside, so they ran back to their van to get shoe covers so they wouldn't track mud on our carpeting.

Aaron was like a surgeon going to work to diagnose the problem. First, he tested the signal and said it was weak. He and Randee carefully inspected every connection and outlet and told me that they wanted to replace every plug. It turns out that the connectors that our electrician had installed were of inferior quality compared to those provided, at no charge, by Time Warner.

While Randee was replacing every plug, Aaron went outside to examine the cable lines. He came back and asked when they had been installed. I explained that we had cable about ten years ago and they were installed at that time.

"You'll get a much stronger signal with our new cables," he said. Then, he headed to the van to get the necessary equipment.

In the meantime, Randee was explaining to me that the $200 power strip I bought to plug in our new TV was not necessary. In fact, they don't even plug the cable wire into it because it interferes with the signal. He suggested I return it for a refund and head to the hardware store to buy a $10 power surge protector. He was right, and he saved me $190 with that suggestion.

When Aaron completed the installation of the outdoor cable, he came inside and hooked up the HD box. He not only taught me how to use the box, he taught me how to use our new TV.

These two fine, young professionals spent more than two hours at our home and got both of our TVs running perfectly. The picture quality and audio was far superior to what it had been. My mom was visiting from out of town and we both enjoyed the personalities and professionalism of Aaron and Randee so much that I invited them to join our family for a spaghetti dinner. They declined but they wished us a Happy New Year and thanked me for the offer.

Five minutes after they left, I called their supervisor, Mark, and left a message on his phone, giving him a glowing report of the exceptional service we had received. His response was the icing on the cake. He called me the next day to thank me for the message. "People don't generally take time to call us when things go well. We usually only hear the complaints," he said. He also told me that he had forwarded my voice mail message to his superiors, including the company president.

Here are the things Aaron and Randee did right:

- ◆ They arrived right on time.

- ◆ Their uniforms were clean and pressed.

- ◆ They greeted us with smiles.

- ◆ They introduced themselves by name and said hello to other family members.

- ◆ They respected our home by covering their shoes each time they came in from outside.

- ◆ They took the time to explain everything they were doing and why.

- ◆ When they called the home office to request hook-up service, they were courteous, friendly and patient with the co-worker who was helping them on the other end of the line.

- ◆ They went the extra mile by giving us money-saving tips and teaching us how to use our new TV.

Never underestimate the effect that one or two employees can have on the way your customers feel about your company. Each employee makes a tremendous difference, as these two gentlemen demonstrated.

Is Your Service
Worth Bragging About?

We had finally embarked on a project that we'd been putting off for 13 years. We decided to have all of our hardwood floors sanded and refinished. The work had to be scheduled in two phases because the project involved three upstairs bedrooms, stairs, a dining room and living room. In short, our whole house would be ripped apart.

The first week was tough because two rooms full of bedroom furniture had to be moved into the third bedroom. Our family spent an entire week sleeping on mattresses and a sofa in our family room. We hired movers to handle the furniture.

The second week was stressful as the movers came back to replace our furniture on freshly finished floors and move our piano into the family room. The guys laid down pads and never made a mark as they moved our heavy dressers and set up two beds. They carefully lifted each piece of furniture for me so that I could apply protective pads to the bottoms of the legs.

They listened carefully as I expressed my concern about a piano being rolled over the new dining room floor. After they briefly discussed the situation, they proceeded to lift the piano and carry it from one end of our house to the other so it never touched the floor.

I was so impressed that, after they left, I called Bill Schmidt (no relation), the owner of Schmidt Moving & Storage Co. Inc., in Milwaukee, Wisconsin.

"You have a fantastic team of employees," I said. "They listened to my concerns, patiently helped me with my tasks and went the extra mile every step of the way. I will recommend your company to everyone I know."

"You made my day," Bill replied. "Thank you for offering to tell others. That's what keeps us in business."

Forget the customer satisfaction surveys. When it boils down to determining customer loyalty, there are only two questions that you need to ask your customers:

- ♦ "Will you do business with us again?"
- ♦ "Will you recommend our business to others?"

If your customers answer "yes" to these questions, thank them profusely. They've just saved the company a fortune in marketing. If your customers answer "no" to the questions, immediately ask them, "Why not?" Then, follow up with a more important question, "What could we have done differently?"

Here are some questions you can ask yourself to get you thinking about whether or not your service is worth bragging about:

- ♦ If this were my business, would I give the same attention to quality and service that I do now?
- ♦ Am I more careful about work quality or customer service when my boss is around?
- ♦ Do I treat every customer like an old friend?
- ♦ Do I deliver good quality and service even when my boss or co-workers do not?
- ♦ Do I actively search for ways to improve service?
- ♦ Do I go beyond my job description?
- ♦ Do I make a special effort to understand each customer's special needs?
- ♦ Can I guarantee that my last 10 customers were satisfied?

Ownership of great service is a necessary ingredient for delivering service that is worth bragging about. It needs to come from each and every employee. Don't wait for your boss to tell you how to treat your customers. Ownership is based on common sense and choosing to do the right thing.

COMMUNITY OUTREACH RAISES MORALE

Handling customer calls and complaints every day can sometimes cause employee burnout. That's why it's important to be on the lookout for ways to maintain a positive work environment. Generosity and community involvement are wonderful ways to raise employee morale in your customer service department.

Bring your employees together for a brainstorming session on how they can "adopt" a cause. Your reps can implement a community outreach program as a team. It can be set it up as a quarterly or monthly program in order to give each employee the opportunity to support his or her favorite cause.

Community outreach does not need to involve a lot of expense. Invite people to share information about their favorite charities or ideas to help individuals in need. Write everyone's ideas on a flip chart. Once all of the ideas have been documented, invite the team to vote on the one they'd like to implement first, second, etc. Then, challenge the team to brainstorm on ways to implement the first idea.

Ideas may include:

♦ **Adopting a family in need during the holidays.** Your team can contact a local volunteer center or church to identify a family. Once that family has been identified, each team member can draw the name and age of a family member. That employee is then responsible for either purchasing or making an age appropriate gift for that individual.

◆ **Delivering food to a local food pantry.**
Each month, your team can hold a food drive. Employees can take turns delivering it to the food pantry.

◆ **Participating in crisis response programs.**
Every year, the American Red Cross is there for hurricane, earthquake, and other disaster victims—including 150 families forced from their homes by fire every day. They offer a variety of outreach opportunities. Your team can sponsor a blood drive or rally to organize personal hygiene packages to be sent to hurricane disaster victims.

When people are involved in outreach and giving, they are thinking of others and feeling good about themselves. Community service does boost employee morale because it instills a spirit of giving and support that carries over into the workplace. Websites such as www.JustGive.org can provide your team with creative ideas and resources for reaching out to others in need.

MANAGE YOUR CUSTOMERS' "MOMENTS OF TRUTH"

Once again, I was having a problem with my laptop computer. First, I looked at the manual to see if I could figure out how to resolve it. The answer wasn't there. But it listed a website that I could visit for troubleshooting advice. When I visited the site, it was very comprehensive but I still couldn't understand the solution. The site listed a toll-free number for technical support. I called the Toshiba technical support line.

I was put on hold for 20 minutes. But I really didn't mind, because it was exactly what I expected. When I called, I was greeted with a recorded message that told me how long the hold time would be. So I simply set my phone on speaker and went about my business. When a rep finally answered, I grabbed the phone and told him about my problem. The scenario I just shared with you represented my own five "moments of truth."

In 1987, Jan Carlzon, the former president of Scandinavian Airlines, wrote a book entitled *Moments of Truth*. A "moment of truth" is any instance in which a customer comes into contact with some aspect of your organization and has an opportunity to form an impression about the quality of service you provide. These moments of truth reflect the customer's experience and each one creates in your customer's mind an image about your entire organization.

Carlzon pointed out that all businesses are judged whenever they interact with their customers. How the phone is answered, the friendliness of the customer service representative, the appearance of an invoice, the receipt of a bill in the mail, company vehicles, advertising, the ease of parking, how orders are packaged, and the cleanliness of a facility—are all moments of truth.

Each moment of truth has impact. It can be positive or negative, but your direct customer interaction, either by telephone or face-to-face, will have the most lasting effects on customer impressions and will produce the most dramatic results. It is therefore extremely important to master your communication skills, both verbal and non-verbal.

Here are the moments of truth I experienced with Toshiba:

♦ **Reviewed the manual for information.**
   The manual was professionally printed, well organized and visually pleasing.

♦ **Visited the website.**
   The Toshiba website is easy to navigate and offers many simple solutions for common technical problems. Contact information was clearly listed and easy to locate.

◆ **Called technical support.**
The recorded message was friendly and brief. Once I selected the option to speak to a technical support representative, I was informed that there was a high volume of calls and given an approximate wait time.

◆ **Spoke with a technical support representative.**
The young man was quite professional and friendly. He explained why he needed the serial number of the computer before he asked for it. I told him what the problem was and he reassured me by saying, "Now don't you worry one bit. I'll help you get it resolved."

"Are you sure?" I asked.

"I won't get off this line until it's fixed. I promise," he said.

◆ **Worked with the rep to resolve the problem.**
The technical support rep walked me through the process step by step with great patience. He used encouraging statements as I stumbled on some of his instructions. Finally, we got the problem resolved.

At each of these "moments of truth," many things can go right or wrong to create a strong impression for the customer about the organization. They are so powerful that positive moments of truth are the building blocks of customer loyalty. More often than not, it is the frontline employees who handle these moments of truth. Managing moments of truth means we need to look at them from both the business level and the human level.

We need to examine how our customers "feel" when they come into contact with our moments of truth.

How do they feel when they read our marketing materials? Are the materials easy to read or do they cause frustration?

How do they feel when they visit our website? Do we waste their time because we've added so much splash and unnecessary graphics that it takes forever to download? Is it easy for them to navigate and find the information they are looking for? Do we hide our contact information so it is difficult for them to find a phone number?

Most importantly, how do our customers feel when they interact with any of our employees? Do they feel like someone genuinely cares about them or do they feel like robots are serving them?

I asked my Toshiba technical support rep where his office was. He told me that he was chatting with me from his office in Istanbul, Turkey. He treated me like an old friend whom he was happy to help. Not once did he sound condescending or impatient with my lack of expertise. Instead, he kept his promise, and my laptop is now working perfectly.

It is up to you to manage moments of truth with your customers. Make a list of the moments of truth when customers come into contact with some aspect of your organization. Don't forget to include your internal customers (co-workers). Then identify ways you can manage these moments to create a more positive experience for the customer.

CUSTOMER SERVICE IS SHOWING OTHERS YOU CARE

It was starting to rain when I checked in for a two-night stay at the Pheasant Run Resort in St. Charles, Illinois. My first night was rough because I was kept awake by some guests who decided to have a party until 2:00 a.m. So, I was tired the next morning when I headed out into the still pouring rain. I was on my way to present a full-day management training seminar. I was worried about my energy level due to lack of sleep, but the seminar attendees were friendly, enthusiastic and engaged. This made the day enjoyable and the time went by quickly.

At the end of day I headed back to my car in the still pouring rain. I called my husband to find out if it was storming in Wisconsin. He said it had been raining hard all day and our entire backyard was under water. I began to stress out about the possibility of our basement flooding.

When I returned to the resort, it was packed with hundreds of college students who were checking in for a large conference. I met Jim Wahl, one of the gentlemen who handle valet services for the guests. He walked across the room to greet me and he asked me how my stay had been so far. I told him I hadn't gotten much sleep the night before and also asked him where I could get a stronger Internet connection for my laptop. I mentioned that the signal in my room was too weak for me to get my work done. He listened carefully and said, "I'm going to try to take care of both of those problems for you."

Within ten minutes after returning to my room, there was a knock on the door. It was Jim. He brought a special adapter that would give me a stronger Internet signal. "Try this," he said. "It's our last one, so hang on to it." Then he told me that he knew the resort was going to be noisy that night so he was working on trying to find me a more quiet room location.

Later that evening, I moved my laptop to the lobby to finish my work. The rain continued to fall. I called home again. The flood news was worse. I was feeling exhausted, missing my family, worrying about the flooding and nervous about the next day's seminar. Jim spotted me and said, "Come on. I'll show you a quieter place where you'll have some peace and receive a good signal." He walked me to a lovely library room where there was soft music playing.

Although he was extremely busy, Jim stopped by a few times to share a warm smile and ask how I was doing. He said, "I'm working with the manager and as soon as things settle down I'll let you know if we've got a room for you."

Around 8 p.m., I went back to my room and tried to relax. I dozed off for a little while. When I awoke, there was a note under my door. Jim had picked up some treats for me including a fruit bowl, cookies and hot chocolate. He had tried to deliver them to my room but was concerned that I was sleeping and didn't want to disturb me. His note said I should dial "0" if I would like him to bring me my snacks. He also apologized because the resort was sold out and he was unable to move me to quieter location.

I was so tired that I never called. It didn't matter to me that I didn't receive the treats or the different room. Jim's empathy, smiles, kind words and gestures made all the difference that evening. I was finally able to relax and trust that everything would turn out all right. I was moved by his sincere concern for my well-being.

Sometimes we get too caught up in thinking about what service is. We get so busy that we forget that service is just about being nice. Customer service is simply kindness. Dare to walk across the room. Get out of your comfort zone and show a customer that you care. Your kindness may help that person in ways you'll never know.

TAKE OWNERSHIP
TO KEEP YOUR CUSTOMERS

My husband, Larry, and I had purchased a very expensive Verlo mattress. From the day it was delivered, Larry was disappointed with the mattress. It seemed to really sag every time he lay down on it. He said he felt like he was "hanging on for dear life" so he wouldn't fall out of bed. For months, we tried everything from flipping and turning the mattress to changing sides on the bed. But the problem continued.

Verlo has a 60-day comfort guarantee where they will come out, pick up the mattress, take it back to the factory and make adjustments until you're comfortable. But we didn't call. We just kept hoping the problem would go away. Finally, 130 days after our purchase, I called the Verlo store and complained about the problem.

A nice young lady named Jennifer patiently listened while I sang the blues. She said, "Although it's well past our service guarantee time frame, I'll arrange for a courtesy adjustment so you won't be charged. However, I'd like you to come into our store tomorrow to try out a few mattresses so you can tell us the firmness you're looking for. I won't be here tomorrow, so please ask for Todd."

The next day when I walked into Verlo, Todd greeted me warmly. He told me he was expecting me. I said, "Todd, I need you to save my marriage. My husband is sleeping in the guest bedroom because he can't stand our new mattress."

Todd said, "Jennifer explained the problem and I looked up your records. I see you have the soft box springs, I'd like to re-place them with a firmer set."

"Do it, Todd!"

"You got it!" Todd said. "Then I'd like to have the factory add some more quilting to firm up the overall mattress."

"Let's do it!"

"Let's go for it!" he said. "And we'll have them reinforce the borders while they're at it so your husband won't feel like he's rolling out. If we pick the mattress up Wednesday morning, it will be all fixed and back to you by 4 p.m. the same day."

I thanked Todd at the Verlo store for demonstrating that he really cared. As I was leaving, he said, "Trust me. Once we get these adjustments made, you'll be delighted that you selected Verlo over the other mattress brands."

He was right!

WIGGLE THE BREAD
TO DELIGHT CUSTOMERS

It was getting too late to go home and cook dinner so I called Cousin's Subs in Glendale to place an order. I figured we could swing through the drive-thru and pick up our sandwiches on the way home. I was put on hold ... forever. I gave up and decided to just head over there to order our subs.

There was only one car in the parking lot and no customers waiting when we walked in. I told the clerk that I had been placed on hold and never got through. She apologized and smiled warmly. Then, her two co-workers came over and apologized. They explained that, 20 minutes earlier, it had been insanely busy.

The manager stood by while I placed my order. He then rushed over to the food preparation area to begin making the sandwiches before the transaction was even completed.

I called to him, "Please make sure the bread is soft. I can't stand it when it's dry."

He jogged over, put on his plastic gloves and began pulling loaves of wheat bread out of the bin. Then, he wiggled each one in the air above his head to show me how fresh and soft they were. Soon, my son and I were giggling with delight. In fact, the other employees and customers who had just walked in were giggling, too.

We gave him the wiggle approval ratings on each loaf and he made our sandwiches out of the loaves we chose. The sandwiches were done in less than five minutes. When we arrived home, we sat down to dinner. The subs were delicious.

I relayed the story to my family and we all agreed ... it's just that easy to build customer loyalty!

DELIVER QUALITY SERVICE...
...BUT HURRY UP!

You're supposed to care deeply about your customers. But you'd better do it at a record-breaking speed. Mixed messages about customer service are commonplace in call centers and they create extreme levels of stress for customer service representatives.

Dealing with contradictory messages presents a real challenge because employees cannot serve two masters at the same time. On the one hand, employees are told to deliver exceptional customer service. On the other hand, their job performance is measured based on productivity—how many calls they handle and the length of each call.

Many customer service representatives attend my training seminars because their managers want them to learn how to build customer loyalty. I teach them the do's and don'ts of customer communications. I encourage them to take time with each customer by actively listening to his or her needs. They learn creative ways to go the extra mile to make their customers happy. They also learn how to turn angry customers into loyal customers.

By the time they've completed the training, most of the employees are fired up and motivated to get back to their call centers and do right by their customers. I'm excited by their enthusiasm. But lately, more employees have been telling me, "I loved this training and agree with everything you've taught us, I just don't think my manager will allow me to do it this way."

"Why not?" I ask.

"Because our performance evaluations are based on how many calls we handle each day, not the quality of the way the call was handled."

Great customer service requires a positive attitude and enthusiastic effort. It sometimes takes more time, but in the end, it saves everyone's time because things get done the right way. Managers need to be cautious about sending mixed messages. If they want employees to deliver quality service that builds customer loyalty, they need to support their employees' efforts.

Here are nine questions to consider when evaluating a call center employee's performance:

1. Does this employee consistently begin each telephone conversation with a warm, friendly greeting?

2. Does this employee use the customer's name at the beginning and end of each conversation?

3. Does this employee patiently listen to his or her customers without interrupting?

4. Does this employee demonstrate proper telephone etiquette?

5. Does this employee follow through on the customer's request to be sure it was completed correctly?

6. Does this employee maintain a solution-oriented attitude when faced with problems or difficult customers?

7. Does this employee use positive communication to show empathy for the customers?

8. Does this employee take ownership of meeting customer needs and resolving customer complaints?

9. Does this employee actively seek ways to do what's best for the customers?

Employees are far more motivated when their performance is measured on how calls are handled, not just how quickly tasks are completed. They'll know that their managers are not just paying lip-service to quality customer service when they are rewarded for taking time and making an effort to build positive relationships with customers. These relationships will result in loyalty, increased customer retention and greater profitability for the company.

TEN SUREFIRE WAYS TO *LOSE* GREAT EMPLOYEES

1. Treat prospective employees with disrespect during the interview process and drag out the application/ interview process too long.

2. Do not return job candidates' phone calls or keep them posted on the status of the job that they are applying for.

3. Tell new employees that they will be a vital part of the "team"; then fail to keep them in the loop when changes are occurring in their department.

4. Do not actively listen to your employees' ideas or act on their suggestions for process improvement.

5. Criticize employees in front of their peers, or, worse, other members of the management team.

6. Do not follow up with employees after they have completed work projects to let them know the final outcome of their efforts.

7. Forget to thank employees for a job well done.

8. Provide customer service training for employees but fail to require upper-level managers to attend or hold them accountable for the same service skills.

9. Focus more of your time and attention on negative employees than you do on your positive, loyal, reliable employees.

10. Give your employees orders with words like "should," "must," and "have to" instead of ASKING them to carry out their duties.

DON'T SKIMP ON TRAINING

It's a proven fact that companies that provide well-planned employee training programs will outperform their competitors. The best companies in the world spend the most on training, so their people are top-notch. You can talk all you want about great customer service or wishing more sales would come in, but until you decide how much you are willing to spend on consistent, quality training, you will never be the best in your industry.

Training does much more than just teach new skills. It sends a message to employees that they are valued by the organization. Training builds positive teamwork and serves as a communication bridge between departments. Training provides a forum for employees to express their views and feel a part of the "Big Picture."

Training should be viewed as an investment in success, rather than as an expense.

The Loyalty Leader®'s Tips for Training

♦ Include training in your annual budget. It's usually determined by a percentage of sales.

♦ Make an ongoing commitment to provide training to employees at all levels of the organization.

♦ Bring in the experts. You know your business best, but training experts will help you improve each area by identifying core issues and recommending training solutions.

♦ Develop a consistent training curriculum—and stick to it!

♦ Require all new employees to participate in an orientation that includes customer service training. Set service standards for all employees. Teach them that *everyone* has customers. Some employees may only deal with internal customers such as co-workers, but they should be required to deliver the same quality of service as employees who deal with the external customers.

- ◆ Mix it up with fresh faces. If the same employee always delivers the training, people stop listening. Involve different employees in the delivery of internal training.

- ◆ Periodically it's good to bring in outside speakers. This can keep training fresh, entertaining, motivational and current. Just like kids, employees tend to get bored when their peers or bosses deliver the training messages. I call this the "Parent Syndrome." Employees are more enthusiastic and receptive to learning when training is delivered from an outsider. The basic messages may be the same, but the trainer is perceived as an expert or authority on the subject.

When You're the Trainer

Here are some tips to help you if you've been asked to teach a class or train a group in your organization:

- ◆ Start by building rapport with the group. Give a brief introduction of yourself, your credentials, and the learning objectives of the meeting. Get the participants involved. Ask them to briefly share their background and what they expect to learn.

- ◆ As you proceed through your material, before making the next point, summarize what you have just covered and link it to the next content piece. Make clear transitions between the major points.

- ◆ Support your teaching with practical examples. Most adults want to know how to apply what you are teaching them. Share real examples of what worked, what didn't go well, and why.

- ◆ Give participants the opportunity to ask questions throughout your presentation. You may need to encourage this by asking, 'What are your questions, concerns or comments about what we have covered so far?

♦   Use common, everyday language. Avoid jargon and clichés.

♦   Nicely wrap up your presentation. Summarize key points and encourage the participants to use what they have learned.

♦   Relax and just be yourself. Use encouraging self-talk and silence the internal critic.

YOUR ROLE IN TRAINING

Every time you are offered the chance to attend a training class or seminar sponsored by your company—take it. But take it further than just showing up and letting the instructor do all the work. Set a goal to learn all you can from the class being offered. The more teachable you are, the greater your chances for success.

Here are some guidelines to help you get the most out of every training class you attend:

♦   Learn and apply the ground rules for the class. Respect the individual styles and needs of every participant.

♦   Take full responsibility for completing any pre-work before the class begins or homework between classes. The more prepared you are, the more you'll learn. Lack of preparation is a time-waster for the class facilitator and other participants.

♦   Stick to the subject that's being discussed to avoid creating confusion for others. Avoid bringing up those fascinating stories that don't support the topic at hand.

♦   Encourage others to participate. People learn best when they discover and verbalize for themselves. Some people are naturally shyer than others, or they may be afraid of making a mistake. When you show a sincere interest in what other class members think and feel, they will be more likely to speak up.

◆ Guard yourself from asking too many questions or talking too much. If you're a person who participates easily, discipline yourself by counting to ten before you open your mouth to speak.

LAUGHTER LEADS THE WAY TO LEARNING

When I think of some of the training seminars I've attended over the years, the movie *Ferris Bueller's Day Off* comes to mind. If you've seen the movie, you will probably remember the scene where all of the students in a history class are so bored their eyes are glazed over. One student has his head on the desk with drool trickling out of his mouth.

Unfortunately, many employees dread attending training workshops for the same reason. They're convinced that the seminars will be a boring and a waste of their valuable time. That's why trainers need to find ways to surprise employees with something they don't expect—FUN!

A common mistake that hurts the credibility of trainers is pretending to know the answer to every question or getting defensive when they don't know. But training will fail miserably when employees are bored. When they're not having fun, they are less likely to learn or retain the information that is being taught. Humor keeps learners engaged in the training, resulting in greater retention of the material and a stronger ability to apply what they've learned when they're back on the job.

When you are responsible for training, use personal stories, self-effacing humor and fun, interactive exercises to keep your participants attentive. They'll forget the bullet points on the slides but will most likely remember the points you made with your stories.

Keep the humor clean, fun and applicable to your material. For example, in my customer loyalty training seminar, I open the class with a funny story about how one of my skirts was ruined by a drycleaner. It gets people laughing and thinking about their own customer service horror stories. My story is the icebreaker that makes it easy for members of the class to engage in a discussion of the characteristics of good and bad service. I ask a few class volunteers to share their own stories and we're off and running.

Sharing your own true stories will be the most effective way to generate laughter and empathy with training participants. Humor creates a rich learning environment. Be sure your stories and exercises support the key information you want the employees to learn.

To make your training more memorable, get them laughing!

500 YEARS OF EXPERIENCE AND STILL LEARNING

Since I present over a hundred workshops and keynote presentations each year, I generally don't get too nervous in front of an audience. But that changed recently when I was invited to present my *How to Deliver Exceptional Internal Customer Service* training workshop to a team of seasoned employees at Northwestern Mutual.

Although there were only 26 employees participating in the workshop, their collective years of employment at this company totaled more than 500 years! Many of them started working there shortly after high school or college and worked their way up through the company for more than 30 years. That's a lot of experience.

My nervousness came from the realization that most of these employees had attended hundreds of classes and workshops over the years. Would they be resistant to learning and have a "know-it-all" attitude? Would they be bored with my material?

As it turned out, my worries were unfounded. Everyone in this group totally surprised and delighted me. They walked in with open minds, positive attitudes and a willingness to learn. Without exception, every individual participated enthusiastically and asked great questions.

After the workshop, I was reflecting on the experience. As I reviewed the evaluations I was deeply moved by the overwhelmingly positive comments they had written. I would love to take all the credit for the success of the training but it's those employees who deserve the credit. You see, I learned more from them that day then they will ever know. Each of those employees demonstrated for me what it means to be a life-long learner. They were wise beyond their years of experience because they recognized that we can all learn something new--every day--if only we're open to learning.

They renewed my commitment to remain open-minded and to listen to others, even children, when they are trying to teach me something. Life-long learners lead much richer lives because they never shut out the opportunities to grow.

EQUIP EMPLOYEES TO
GO THE EXTRA MILE

While standing in the checkout line at a grocery store, I observed a customer interaction that drove me crazy. The clerk told an elderly woman she had written her check for twenty cents more than the amount due. The woman informed him that it was the amount on the receipt.

"Oh, then I guess it was my fault," the clerk said.

The customer replied, "No problem. Just give me the twenty cents and I'll be on my way."

The clerk said, "I'm not allowed to do that. You'll have to go to the customer service desk to get your money."

The customer replied, "You must be kidding. You mean I have to walk to the other side of the store and stand in line to get the twenty cents I'm owed as a result of your mistake?"

About this time, the young clerk noticed I was glaring at him. He reached in his drawer, handed the woman two dimes and said, "I guess I'll just deal with it later."

My son said to him, "You're lucky you did that or my mom would write about you in her newsletter!"

I'd be willing to bet that you have had a similar experience. This is the kind of thing that happens when employees are not given the power to do the right thing for their customers.

Forget the mission statement and start focusing on empowerment—not just the concept, but letting your employees take charge. They can only do this with sufficient training.

Puttin' on The Ritz...

The Ritz-Carlton Hotel Company's training managers and senior hotel executives give personal, two-day demonstrations of "Gold Standards" to all new employees. Three weeks later, the orientation units reconvene for follow-up sessions, after which the employees are considered "Ladies or Gentlemen at The Ritz-Carlton."

To cultivate customer loyalty, Ritz-Carlton Hotels has a rule: "Any employee who receives a guest complaint owns the complaint." The hotel chain makes a commitment to teaching employees *how* to provide world-class service. First-year managers and employees receive 250 to 310 hours of training.

After they have completed initial training, first-line employees such as housekeeping, busboys, etc., have the authority to spend up to $2,000 to immediately correct a problem or handle a complaint. Managers can spend up to $5,000. Now that's empowerment.

At every level, The Ritz-Carlton is detail-oriented. Steps for all quality-improvement and problem-solving procedures are documented, through data collection and analysis.

For example, to meet its goal of total elimination of problems, The Ritz-Carlton has determined that there are 970 potential instances for a problem to arise during interactions with overnight guests and 1,071 such instances during interactions with meeting event planners.

Customer service standards have been established for every single instance and every employee has been trained and empowered to uphold those standards.

Ritz-Carlton officials know this will create a win-win-win situation. The employee feels good about himself, the guest is happy, and the company will keep the business. In an independent survey, 99 percent of guests said they were satisfied with their Ritz-Carlton experience; more than 80 percent were "extremely satisfied."

Ritz-Carlton management works hard to create loyal employees and customers by making them feel valued. It's just a matter of going the extra mile. After all, that's what Loyalty Leaders do!

THE LOYALTY ALPHABET

A few years ago, I presented a program on customer loyalty for more than 165 employees who work at community banks surrounding the Madison, Wisconsin area.

Kim Kahl, training coordinator for State Bank of Cross Plains, wanted to encourage individuals from the various banks to meet and network with new people rather than sitting with their co-workers. On each nametag, she wrote a letter of the alphabet that corresponded with a table. On each table, she displayed a customer service tip that started with that letter. For example, my nametag had the letter "**J**" on it so I was seated at the "jargon" table.

I loved her idea and the great customer service tips her team came up with for each letter of the alphabet. Kim was kind enough to let me share them with you. Her table tent displays were a terrific way to reinforce the customer service principles I taught in my program.

Here is the customer service alphabet developed by Kim and her team:

A	Attitude
B	Body language
C	Courteous
D	Dedicated
E	Eye contact
F	Friendly
G	Greet your customer
H	Handshake
I	Introduce yourself
J	[Avoid] Jargon when communicating with customers

K	[Customer service is] Key
L	Listen
M	Make their day!
N	[Identify] Needs
O	Opportunities
P	Product knowledge
Q	Questions: Asking the "right" questions
R	[Customer] Retention
S	Service with a Smile!
T	Thanks for your business!
U	Upbeat
V	Vow to deliver quality service
W	What else can I help you with today?
X	X-selling (cross-selling)
Y	You can make a difference!
Z	Zero in on customer needs

GET TO KNOW YOUR CO-WORKERS

My husband and son like to tease me whenever we play a game of backyard baseball. It seems I've never learned the proper way to throw a ball. No matter how patiently they coach me, I still don't get it. Every time I throw, the ball either goes way out of the yard or straight into the dirt. Sometimes they encourage me to throw a ball just so they can have a good laugh (at my expense).

On the flip-side, my husband can't carry a tune to save his life. His voice squeaks and grinds as he jumps between octaves. He gets bewildered glances from fellow worshippers every time he sings hymns in church. At home, we sometimes encourage him to belt out a tune from *The Sound of Music* just so we can have a good laugh (at his expense).

My husband is talented at baseball and I can carry a tune. While we were chatting one night about our unique talents, I was reminded of the wide range of talents present on every team of employees. Yet, we often fail to recognize these talents because we focus on an individual's failings instead of taking time to learn about his or her strengths.

Here's one exercise I use when I facilitate team-building seminars for my clients. I tell everyone on the team to select a partner. They are encouraged to choose the person they know the least about. Using a timer, the employees are given one minute to tell their partner about a unique talent or interest they may have. They can talk about something they accomplished when they were younger, something unique about their family or background, an activity they're currently involved in, or even a dream they have about their future.

While each person is speaking, his or her partner must practice active listening to try to remember as many details as possible. After the minute is up, they switch roles.

This exercise was originally designed to teach employees about active listening, but an amazing thing started to happen. They did learn more about listening skills, but more importantly they started learning about each other on a different level. Many employees discovered common interests that created an instant rapport.

For example, here were some discoveries made during various classes:

- ◆ Two employees discovered they were singers and members of two different choral groups that perform on weekends. Prior to this, they had barely talked to each other working side by side in their department. Now they go to lunch together and chat about what's going on with their singing careers.

- ◆ Three employees from one team had military backgrounds and discovered that they had a mutual interest in the National Guard.

- ◆ One employee had extensive computer expertise that his manager was unaware of. It dramatically changed his co-workers' perception of his abilities. As a result, his role in the department was expanded to tap into his passion and knowledge of computers.

I've observed employees discovering mutual interests about travel destinations, gourmet cooking, volunteerism, community groups, and much more. During the 15-minute break after this exercise, a buzz of conversation takes place between employees who had worked together for years but barely knew one another.

Getting to know your co-workers at a deeper level and learning about their unique talents or interests can build rapport and mutual respect. Recognizing these talents will help you to focus on the positive aspects of the individuals you work with on a daily basis.

SEVEN WAYS TO BUILD LOYALTY WITH YOUR CO-WORKERS

1.   When you make a promise to a co-worker—keep it!

2.   Explain your co-workers' absences in a positive light. Customers do not need to know they are in the restroom or on a break.

3.   Your co-workers are your #1 customers. Give them the same caring service that you give to your external customers.

4.   Follow-up with co-workers to let them know the outcome of a service request that they had to forward to you for completion.

5.   Frequently compliment and thank your co-workers for a job well done—in front of other people. Be sure you're sincere!

6.   Take complete, legible messages for your co-workers so they can be prepared when they return their calls.

7.   Witty or sarcastic remarks that roll off your tongue could hurt the feelings of a co-worker. Remember the golden rule!

EMPLOYEE ATTITUDE ADJUSTMENTS

A CEO of a large company once asked me to give him tips on how he could improve the attitudes of his employees. He said that he was concerned because it seemed like negative attitudes were permeating throughout many of the company's departments. I told him that if he is noticing those attitudes, so are his customers.

Here are the five steps I suggested he implement to begin improving employee attitudes:

1.   As you hire new employees, focus primarily on their attitudes, not just their skills. Most skills can be taught, attitudes cannot. Pay very careful attention to the demeanor, attitude and enthusiasm of job candidates. If there is even the slightest doubt in your mind about their sincerity— don't hire them.

2.   Seriously consider terminating employees who continue to be extremely negative even after they have been given several opportunities to improve their behavior. Attitudes are contagious. No matter how productive an employee is, consistently negative behavior such as criticizing co-workers or the company can take down the morale of an entire work team.

3.   The CEO, president or owner needs to reserve two hours per week to visit employees throughout the company and personally meet them and acknowledge their individual efforts. Do not schedule the visits for the same time each week, or they will become predictable and lose their impact. Take time to chat for a few minutes with each of your employees, and be sure to listen to their suggestions. Sincerity is a must!

4.   Hold employees, particularly senior managers, accountable for their attitudes and behavior toward their co-workers. Require all managers to attend customer service training programs along with their employees.

5.   Thank your employees every chance you get. Hand-written notes, personal comments or phone calls to employees are effective methods for improving internal attitudes. They are also more powerful tools for building loyalty than carefully planned employee recognition programs.

How to Handle Bitter Employees

Do you have employees who are cynical and constantly complaining about their job and company to their co-workers? Perhaps they have been employed at the company for many years and are good workers. Here is a method that some of my clients have used to turn the situation around.

One employee's negative attitude is highly contagious and can seriously damage the morale of an entire work team. What's worse, managers who coddle these individuals send a powerful message to the rest of the team, "It's OK to be cynical and even disrespectful as long as you do your job." These are the same managers who lose the respect of the employees who are doing a great job *and* have a positive attitude toward the company.

Every employee within an organization must be held accountable for his or her behavior. It is unprofessional for any member of the staff to exhibit behavior that is verbally disruptive or destructive to other members of the team. Anger and hostility are forms of manipulation. These are unacceptable workplace behaviors and should not be tolerated in any employee at any level.

Here's what you can do if your constructive feedback and warnings have failed. Be sure you discuss this plan with your Human Resources director, and you have his or her support before you take these steps:

♦   Tell offending employees that you are giving them a "gift" of a paid Friday off. However, they must use this day to carefully think about whether or not they would like to continue working at this company. Tell them that their cynicism is unprofessional and will no longer be tolerated, but because you respect their work, you will give them an opportunity to turn their attitudes around. Give them two options:

- *If they choose to continue their employment, they need to come to work on Monday morning with a*

> *typed contract outlining the specific steps they will take to turn their attitude around to become positive team players.*
>
> • *If they choose not to take ownership of their attitude, then they can either turn in a letter of resignation or be terminated.*

Remember, employee respect is earned. To be an effective manager, you need to treat each member of your staff with equal fairness. This cannot be accomplished when we wear blinders to avoid dealing with the bad apples!

PSST! GOSSIPS CAN BE FIRED

Employees who are gossips can be put on 90-day probation or even fired, according to an article by Harry Wessel. He points out that it is perfectly legal to fire an employee for a bad attitude or gossiping unless there is a union or employment contract setting forth rules on how and under what circumstances workers can be fired. Florida has an "Employment-At-Will" doctrine, which lets companies dismiss workers for any reason.

Gossip can seriously undermine the effectiveness of workplace relationships. There appears to be an increase in workplace gossip, associated with the ongoing restructuring taking place within businesses. As people are working longer hours and coping with an informal communication grapevine, the fine line between what is ethical business information and what is unethical gossip is weakening.

If you venture into the gossip zone, be ready to be responsible for creating friction, upheaval and unnecessary anxiety for those who will ultimately get caught in the web you create. It is very difficult to avoid being involved in daily gossip. Personal talk about someone or an employer has become part of the way many people communicate. But once something has been said, it can't be taken back.

Try practicing gossip avoidance strategies. These strategies will save you time, increase your energy and keep you from hurting someone you work with. Constant workplace change breeds gossip and reduces our energy, respect and credibility. Avoiding gossip means taking a close look at how you currently become involved in gossip. Ask yourself these questions:

1.   Do I initiate discussions about my co-workers job performance or personal lives?

2.   Do I initiate discussions based on second hand information?

3.   Do I consider the comments I make about others to be of real value to the workplace culture and environment?

4.   Do I repeat personal conversations?

5.   Can I be trusted to 'keep' a confidential conversation?

6.   Do I sometimes give confidential information to another because I feel as their 'friend' they should know?

How did you score? Do you need to review your involvement in gossip? You may need to change a few things.

A good technique to start with is to figure out what percentage of your day you currently spend in or around the gossip grapevine. Let's say you spend ten percent of your working day on gossip-related communications. These could be in the form of face-to-face conversations, emails, or telephone conversations. Over the next two weeks gradually reduce that percentage each day. You can do this by gradually cutting out the emails, then the telephone sessions and so on.

Face-to-face gossip is the most difficult area to reduce, particularly if you find it easy to get hooked into your peer group when gossip is on. Attempt to shift the gossip to focus on the business objectives. Try to comment only on the issues and not personal or 'hear-say' information. If the pressure is on, simply excuse yourself from the "gossip zone" and get back to work.

When you can avoid getting "hooked" by gossip, you will earn the respect of others and be viewed as a trusted team member.

A CASUAL DRESS CODE CAN FASHION A SLOPPY IMAGE

It was time for my spring pedicure so I booked an appointment at a local salon. When I arrived, a well-dressed receptionist greeted me and introduced me to my nail technician. She invited me to follow her up a flight of stairs to the spa. My view was embarrassing as her low-rider capris parted ways with her short sweater. Because I was right behind her, I had to look straight down at the steps in order to avoid seeing things that I really didn't want to see.

A few days later, I stopped for a cup of coffee. The young woman at the counter leaned over to hand me my drink. Her sweater was cut so low that everything, and I mean everything from her waist up was exposed. The woman behind me had her 5-year-old son standing with her. She quickly spun him around so he wouldn't see the cashier's bare anatomy.

Even in corporate settings, unclear or unenforced casual dress code policies are being interpreted as opportunities to dress inappropriately. Dress code abuse has caused companies to ban such items as halter tops, stretch pants, jeans, shorts, sandals, and shirts without collars.

Another potential problem with casual office attire is that employees may tend to take work less seriously when they are dressed casually. A survey of managers conducted by the employment law firm Jackson Lewis and cited in Entrepreneur indicated that 44 percent noticed an increase in employee absenteeism and tardiness when casual dress policies were introduced. The managers also noted a rise in inappropriate, flirtatious behavior.

Problems arise when companies define their dress codes using vague words like "appropriate," "professional," and "businesslike" without spelling out a specific policy. This can create confusion among employees. In order to avoid this situation, business owners and managers should spell out their dress codes clearly.

When it comes to professional image and building customer loyalty, clothes do make a difference. Here are some fashion alerts to keep in mind if you want to maintain a professional image:

- Clothing that is too tight is never flattering.

- Clothing that is too revealing makes your co-workers and customers uncomfortable.

- Baggy clothes make you look sloppy and unprofessional.

- Shorts or too-short skirts can make others perceive you as overly casual.

- Gym attire such as yoga pants, t-shirts and running shoes can send the message that you are not serious about your work.

- Others may perceive ripped, wrinkled, torn or dirty clothing as apathy.

People who are serious about climbing the career ladder often choose not to wear casual office attire because they are concerned about their credibility. Bosses may lose the respect of their employees by dressing too casually. Employees may lose out on promotions that go to their better-dressed co-workers. Salespeople risk feeling embarrassed if a customer drops by the office and finds them wearing casual clothing. A good rule of thumb to follow is always dress as well as your best customers.

As the saying goes, "You never get a second chance to make a first impression."

SELF-ASSESSMENT

NAUGHTY OR NICE?
CHECK YOUR LIST TWICE

Being nice is the best customer service and co-worker treatment there is. It doesn't cost much, and it can pay big time. People like to work and do business with people they like.

It's easy to be nice to others when they're being nice to you. But it's quite another story when the other person is rude or cold. When you find yourself dealing with unpleasant customers, rude co-workers or an ineffective boss, ask yourself, "Am I being naughty or nice?"

In other words, are you choosing to rise above the situation or lowering yourself to the level of the unpleasant person? It's unlikely that you'll be able to change the behavior of an unpleas-ant customer or co-worker, but you can change how you choose to respond to others. In order to change your response, you need to first assess your own behaviors.

Check your naughty list below in this self-assessment (each check is a "yes" answer):

- ❏ I give other people too much power by allowing their behavior to dictate how I feel.

- ❏ I get defensive when others verbally attack me or the company for which I work.

- ❏ I speak disrespectfully to others about a co-worker, boss or customer I don't like.

- ❏ I participate in the workplace gossip chain.

- ❏ I sometimes act rudely toward others when I'm tired, stressed or not in the mood to be nice.

Now check your nice list:

- ❏ I put myself in my customer or co-worker's place and try to understand how he or she feels.

❑ I show my co-workers and customers I care through simple acts of kindness.

❑ I am patient when someone is asking me for help, even when I think they should know how to do the activity.

❑ I listen carefully so I don't jump to conclusions about what the other person needs.

❑ I smile often and let people know that I'm approachable.

❑ I jump in to help customers, even when it's not my job.

❑ I am supportive and encouraging to my co-workers.

❑ I treat my boss with respect, even though I may not agree with the way he or she does things.

The quality of customer service cannot exceed the quality of the person who delivers the service. You can establish your own reputation of quality by refusing to react to negative people. When in doubt, choose the "nice" road by following these guidelines:

◆ Customers are not always right, but great service is.

◆ Co-workers are not always right, but kindness is.

◆ Bosses are not always right, but respect is.

Especially during busy seasons like the holidays, when everyone is hurried, practice being especially nice. Greet everyone with a smile. You might make someone's day a little brighter, including yours.

CHAPTER 5

COMMUNICATING WITH CUSTOMERS

The more high tech the world becomes, the more people crave high-touch service.

— John Naisbett, *Megatrends*

The dollar bills the customer gets from the teller in four banks are the same; what's different are the tellers.

— Unknown

FAX ME A COPY OF YOUR FACIAL EXPRESSION

It's faceless, untouchable and remote, yet it's the first moment of truth that your customers have with your company. A telephone can be an excellent marketing tool, or it can damage your customer relationships in ways you'll never know, because your frustrated customers will just silently go away.

You are the voice of your company. Even if you don't have control over how a call is initially answered, make sure that when a call does get to your department it is handled well.

When communicating by telephone, your choice of words is far less important than the tone of your message. You can test this out by saying "Thank you for bringing this to my attention" in four different tones.

Say these same words, but each time change your tone to:

1. angry 2. happy 3. skeptical 4. stressed

Now say "Thank you for bringing this to my attention" in a happy, caring tone of voice but at the same time, cross your arms, scowl, slouch and look down. It's difficult to convey a positive tone. Your body language will negatively impact your tone even when you think you're sounding friendly.

Here are five tips for improving your telephone communications:

1. Use a telephone headset in order to communicate freely with your hands and body.

2. Sit up straight. When you slouch in your chair, your voice will send a message of apathy to your customers.

3. Make sure the expression on your face is a pleasant one. A smile on your face puts a smile in your voice.

4. If you don't have a headset, avoid cradling the telephone receiver between your ear and shoulder. It'll muffle the tone of your voice and make you come across as less trustworthy.

5. Be sure to include a greeting—even when you're busy. Avoid answering your phone abruptly, for instance by saying, "Billing Department, please hold." Instead, say, "Hello, my name is...first."

Use appropriate filler words to replace body language. Your caller does not have the benefit of eye contact, a smile or nod of the head to reassure them that you are still listening. The use of filler words such as, "I understand," "yes," or even "wow" lets your caller know that you are actively listening. Then your customer won't need to ask, "Are you still there?"

Get together with your team to discuss customer expectations, how to manage first impressions and techniques for showing your customers you care. Sometimes in your desire to handle customer conversations as quickly as possible, you can neglect the use of common acknowledgments as you communicate. Yet the few extra seconds it takes to add them is well worth the time. If you simply focus on getting the task done and rush through service requests, you will miss tremendous opportunities to build customer loyalty.

CHATTING WITH CUSTOMERS IS NOT A WASTE OF TIME

I walked into a bakery one morning to buy some bread and was greeted by an employee with a pasted-on smile. As if to apologize for my need to wait, she rolled her eyes at me when the customer in front of me couldn't make up her mind about what to order. When it was my turn, she was all business with efficiency and a small dose of friendliness.

As I was preparing to leave, another employee gave me a great big smile. She said, "I see you in here all the time and I don't even know your name."

"It's Deb."

She replied, "Hi, Deb. It's good to meet you. My name is Pam. By the way, your nails are just beautiful." I thanked her for the compliment and we proceeded to chat for a few minutes.

She asked me what I do for a living and seemed excited to learn a little about my business. Her greeting and our chat completely changed my experience. I know that I'll remember her name and she's the person I'll ask for the next time I shop there.

Customers are people. Just like you, they have families, friends, interests, careers, fears and dreams. Sometimes they want to talk about these things, even with strangers.

Unfortunately, some managers feel that chatting with customers is a waste of time. They tell their employees to focus on productivity instead of relationship building. This is a huge mistake. It's a proven fact that high-growth companies know their customers well and encourage customer communication.

Your customers often tell you way more than you need to know. You may hear about their Uncle Joe's hernia operation, their Las Vegas vacation, their new puppy's cute trick and their children's accomplishments. These customers are sending you a clear message when they share these snapshots of their lives. They are telling you they trust you enough to care.

Listen carefully to your chatty customers and acknowledge what they have said. The more you know about your customers, the stronger the connection they will have with you and your company. In addition to learning about their personal interests, you are also making it safe for them to share other information that is vital to building customer loyalty.

The missing link in quality service delivery is the emphasis on productivity over chatting with customers. Don't forget that making customers feel good about doing business with you increases not only sales but productivity as well. Chatting is a wonderful way to learn about your customer's preferences, needs and expectations. This two-way communication is a key component for building trust.

Follow your customers' cues. If they seem stressed or in a hurry, this is not the time to get chatty. But if they initiate a conversation or respond warmly to your compliment or question, don't rush your service. View this chat time as an investment in strengthening a customer relationship that will translate into greater sales, referrals and, yes, even productivity.

SMILE! IT INCREASES YOUR FACE VALUE

According to psychologists, people aren't happy because they are successful. They are successful because they're happy. Happy people are easier to work with, more highly motivated and more willing to tackle a difficult project. The main reason people get fired isn't incompetence or unreliability; it's that they can't get along with their colleagues.

People can choose to be happy. Happiness comes from within. It does not come from external factors such as success, popularity and possessions. Just take a look at all of the truly miserable celebrities. The first step to happiness is to make the choice that you want to be happy.

If you tend to be a negative person, identify a person whom you like and respect and exhibits a positive outlook on life. Use this person as a role model and practice being happy by modeling your behaviors after theirs.

Smiling can and does impact your life. There's an old saying, "Smile. It increases your face value." It also increases your success. Researchers conclude that people who frequently smile appear to be more successful than their less-happy peers in three primary areas of life: work, relationships and health. This means smiling even when you don't feel like it, because the sheer act of smiling will make you feel happier.

Think about this for a moment. The real value in a smile is when it is given freely to everyone you come in contact with during the day. What value is a smile held back? It immediately becomes worthless to both you and the possible receiver.

There are many opportunities for you to smile in the workplace but you may be missing them due to a heavy workload.

Smile ...

- ◆   when you walk through the door every morning
- ◆   when you record your voice mail message
- ◆   when you leave a voice mail message
- ◆   every time you pick up the phone to place or answer a call
- ◆   when a co-worker interrupts you with a question
- ◆   when the boss tells you to do something you don't want to do

You are probably multi-tasking when you're at work, juggling phone calls, paperwork, emails and more. Each one of these tasks takes time. Smiling takes no time at all! But for some it takes practice. You may need to remind yourself to smile so stick a sign on your desk that reads:

"I am never too busy to smile!"

Perhaps you are smiling right now. If so, you just gave yourself and everyone around you a wonderful gift.

SHIFT INTO NEUTRAL BEFORE TALKING TO CUSTOMERS

I frequently stress the importance of maintaining a positive attitude. After all, attitudes are contagious and being friendly is always the right thing to do when it comes to communicating with your customers and co-workers. But it's not always easy. At times, it's downright difficult to be nice.

As the saying goes, "Life is what happens to you when you're making other plans." During the course of a day, you may be thrown a curveball that can quickly shift your mood from friendly to foul:

- ♦ Road construction holds you up on the way to work and you are literally running through the building in order to make it to your desk by starting time.

- ♦ Your boss stops by at 8:30 a.m. and tells you he wants to meet with you before lunch. He doesn't look happy. Your mind and heart start racing, wondering what it is that you've done wrong.

- ♦ A customer screams at you on the phone, blaming you for the fact that his order is messed up.

- ♦ Your spouse calls to tell you that the plumbing in the bathroom is leaking and there's water all over the floor.

- ♦ You get a call from your son's school. He has a fever and needs to be picked up as soon as possible.

So the question begs to be asked, "Is it okay to be rude or a little nasty to your customers or co-workers when something is going wrong in your life?"

The answer is quite simple, "Absolutely not!"

Think about your own experiences when you are a customer. Do you want to deal with someone who is moody or rude? Do you want to hear about his or her personal problems? Do you want to observe an employee arguing with a co-worker?

You probably answered "no" to the above questions. When you are conducting business, you want the focus to be on your needs and you want to deal with a pleasant person.

Your customers are no different than you. They expect and deserve to conduct business with positive people. Keep in mind that when I refer to customers, I'm also referring to your co-workers. The people you work with day in and day out are your primary customers. If you work full-time, you probably spend more time with your co-workers each week than you spend with your own family. Your attitude can significantly impact the quality of the workplace for everyone. You owe it to your customers and co-workers to have a positive attitude in spite of what is going on in your own life.

If you're going through a challenging time, you can share your fears or frustrations with your close friends at work and seek support. But you need to be careful that complaining, moodiness or anger don't show up as daily habits. Your attitude will become your personal signature. It's what you'll become known for and that can shape your future in a positive or negative way.

Because you are a professional, you need to learn how to shift your mood into neutral. Then you'll be ready to quickly shift into "positive" before you communicate with your customers and co-workers.

How to Shift From Negative to Neutral:

- ◆ Go to the bathroom or an empty conference room and hide out for a few minutes.

- ◆ Splash cool water on your face.

- ◆ Rub your temples and forehead to relax your facial muscles.

- Have a cup of herbal tea. The non-caffeinated warmth will calm you down.

- Go for a 10-minute walk outside during your lunch break.

- Eat a piece of fruit or protein such as a hard-boiled egg.

- Do some deep breathing exercises to quiet your thoughts.

- Stand up and do a few stretching exercises.

COMMUNICATION CHAMPIONS

Eighty-five percent of a person's career success is in direct proportion to his or her communication skills.

- 7 percent are the words we choose

- 33 percent is our voice quality

- 45 percent is our behavior—body language, eye contact and mannerisms

Here are some common actions that create communication barriers:

- Eye rolling

- Sighing

- Rapid-fire foot tapping and leg bouncing or "sewing machine knee"

- Interrupting

- Glancing away from the person who is speaking even for a split second

♦ Excessive head nodding—I call this the "Chihuahua in the window" syndrome

We are often unaware of our body language because it is comprised of subtle habits that we have developed over the years. Our body language sends non-verbal cues that speak volumes.

Do you know what messages your body language is sending? If not, ask your significant other, close friend or a trusted co-worker to tell you which of your behaviors might be annoying to others. It will help you to improve your communication style for better rapport and understanding.

MAGIC WORDS YOUR CUSTOMERS WANT TO HEAR

Customer service works like magic. When it's done well, you magically keep more customers, they magically refer new customers and sales magically go up. When it's done poorly, customers magically disappear.

There are certain magic phrases that let your customers know you are sincere about delivering great service, but the words need to be supported by actions.

"Thank you for calling."

Does your tone tell customers that you truly appreciate their calls? Treat each caller as you would an old friend. Your customer needs to know that you are truly delighted that he or she called. If customers feel like a number or an interruption, they will be less likely to call again.

"How can I help?"

This open-ended question creates an opportunity for your customers to tell you what they need. You're emphasizing the fact that you are there to help, not sell. It also shows your customers that you are willing to listen.

"I can solve the problem."

This lets your customers know that you are solution-oriented and are willing to do what it takes to make them happy.

"You can count on it."

This gives your customers confidence. They want to know that the person who is handling their request is capable, reliable and committed to delivering what's been promised.

"I appreciate your business."

This involves more than a simple "thank you." Genuine appreciation is demonstrated by patiently answering questions, follow-up calls to keep customers posted on the status of their orders, inviting feedback and looking for opportunities to provide value-added service.

TELL YOUR CUSTOMERS "WHY" BEFORE "WHAT"

There are times when you must say "no" to a customer because of a policy that must be enforced. Sometimes you can only provide a service after the customer takes necessary steps such as completing paperwork or sending information to your company. In these situations, customers may get angry or defensive because you can't do what they have requested, or because you have asked them to take action. When you need to say "can't," "won't," or "don't" to your customers' requests, they may ask "Why not?" or worse, "Who can?"

Never fear! By using the simple technique of telling "why" before "what," you can build loyalty even when you can't honor your customers' service requests. This is also a valuable technique when you are providing information, asking someone for information or asking someone to take action.

You'll know your customers are frustrated when they begin to ask questions or make comments such as:

"Why do you need that information?"
"Why do I have to send that in?"
"Why can't you do what I've requested?"
"If you can't take care of this, let me talk to someone who can!"

Telling "why before what" is simply explaining to your customers the reasons for a policy or rule before you tell them you can't do what they have requested. For example:

"Due to federal regulations I am unable to make the changes you have requested, but here are some other options that are available to you."

This technique saves your customers time. Explaining why you need information can make you more efficient because customers will more readily provide the information if they understand why it's needed. This can speed up the service process. For example:

"We ask for your insurance card at every visit because it helps us to keep your insurance information up-to-date. This reduces confusion and saves you time and money when we submit your medical claims."

Telling "why before what" helps your customers. You can build rapport and trust by providing the reasoning behind policies and procedures that aren't immediately evident. When your customers know and understand why something has to be done a certain way, it will also help them be prepared the next time they have a similar situation.

MAKE FRIENDS WITH YOUR CUSTOMERS THROUGH POSITIVE STATEMENTS

If a customer calls and says, "I saw the coolest software while I was at a convention in Las Vegas and I'm interested in ordering it," don't immediately ask the brand and type of computer for which it's needed. Instead talk about the convention in Las Vegas for a couple of minutes and ask what the customer liked about the software. Then you can go into the details of the actual software he would like to order.

If a customer comes into your bank and says, "I need to transfer money from my savings to checking account because we're remodeling the house and I have to pay the contractor," ask her about the remodeling project, and then transfer the funds.

If you're going to spend time on the phone or on the floor dealing with customers, you might as well have some fun. Better yet, why not make it fun for your customers to do business with you?

Make it your personal goal to make friends with your customers by showing interest in their interests, praising them, complimenting them, and making them feel good.

"Your children are so well-behaved," you might say, or "Your remodeling project sounds like it's going to be beautiful," or "You have a such pleasant voice on the phone."

When you make these types of statements, you reinforce your customer's feelings of self-worth. No matter how good your products or marketing may be, business success or failure is often determined simply by how customers are treated.

Here are more examples of positive statements:

- ◆ "Mr. Jackson, thank you for being so patient. I'm sorry for the delay because I know that nobody likes to be kept waiting."

- ◆ "Mrs. Schmidt, welcome home. How was your trip to Hawaii?"

- ◆ "Thank you for placing your order with us. We appreciate and value the fact that you choose to do business with us."

- ◆ "I'm delighted to hear from you every time you call!"

Avoid communications that serve only to annoy customers. Here are some examples of negative statements:

- ◆ "We're very busy right now. Can you call back later?"

- ◆ "I'm with another customer; you'll just have to wait."

- ◆ "I don't know. I don't work in this department."

- ◆ "You'll just have to be patient. We're short-staffed today."

Learn to use positive verbal and non-verbal communication to make your customers feel good about doing business with you and your company. Make customer recognition and praise a consistent element of your service delivery.

GOOFY CUSTOMERS ... GALLANT SERVICE

Standing before the librarian with a self-righteous smirk on my face, I insisted that I had definitely returned the book for which they were trying to charge me a fine. I rambled on and on, explaining how I never lose books, how I'm an extremely organized person, how I had searched everywhere, and how it must be the library's mistake.

Three days later we found the book in a bag attached to my bicycle. It had been in there since last summer.

I sheepishly returned the book. The librarian giggled and winked at me and said, "Don't feel bad. I once lost a book for a whole year. We found it inside a magazine in the pocket behind the driver's seat of my car."

* * *

Sitting in my car at the bank drive-through, I impatiently tapped the steering wheel wondering just why it was taking so long just to deposit a check and send me the $100 in cash I had requested.

I forgot that I had written "For Deposit Only" on the back of the check, which means they must deposit the full amount.

When the teller returned, he apologized for the delay and kindly suggested that I endorse the check with just my name in the future if I want cash back.

Because of my error, he had to go into the bank, find a manager and get special authorization to give me the cash. He did all this because he recognized me and was trying to do me a favor.

In both situations I was the goofy customer who made the mistakes. But I was still treated with gallant service.

Our customers will make mistakes and do goofy things, but when this occurs it is not up to us to teach them a lesson or scold them. We are not in business to judge the behaviors of others, but rather to forgive their mistakes and do the best we can to provide great service. After all, it's what we hope they will do when we mistakes, isn't it?

PUT DOWN THE MOUSE AND PICK UP THE PHONE

Email is a great communication tool, right? Wrong! Email is doing more damage to customer and co-worker relationships than any form of communication. The quality of customer service is on the decline because employees are avoiding face-to-face and even phone conversations. They're hiding behind email.

Email is also lowering productivity in the workplace. The more email you send, the more you get. Managers at one company in Liverpool, England, estimate that its 6,000 employees send each other 40,000 messages a day. Employees everywhere are reporting that they are spending two hours per day dealing with email.

Typically, you can accomplish more in placing a one-minute phone call then you can in sending multiple emails. Conversations give you the opportunity to clarify and build rapport. So, whenever possible, put down your mouse and pick up the phone.

Here are just a few of the negative consequences when employees send email instead of talking to one another or their customers:

◆   There is increased gossip and mistrust.

◆   Issues are not addressed and resolved quickly.

◆   Silos are formed creating an "us vs. them" work environment.

◆   Co-worker empathy decreases because employees are simply not getting to know each other.

◆   Customers are frustrated because they don't get to actually voice their needs or concerns.

◆   Face-to-face or phone conversations convey a warmer, friendlier tone. Email is perceived as being cold and impersonal.

- There is frequent miscommunication and misunderstanding.

Business leaders all over the world are concerned about email over-use and abuse and are taking a stand. "Never on Friday" is becoming a common theme where all internal email is banned every Friday. Ironically, one executive sent an email to employees announcing the Friday email ban. He said he looked forward to not hearing from his employees via email but encouraged them to stop by often.

You can establish a "no email" policy one day a week, even if your company doesn't support an email ban:

- Meet with your co-workers face to face.

- If your customers request email communication, you can still call them to confirm that their information has been sent. Even a voice mail message will help to build a stronger customer relationship. For example: *"Per your request I have emailed the information about your order. Please let me know if you have any questions or need additional information."*

- Pick up the phone and call someone—a customer, co-worker or vendor.

- Get up and walk to another department to chat with members of the team with whom you deal.

- In sales? Get out to the field and meet with your customers.

You could take the idea a step farther by introducing other "no technology" days, such as no cell phones on Monday, no PDAs on Tuesday, no web surfing on Wednesdays, and no memos on Thursday.

Imagine: people might actually start talking to one another again!

EMAIL ETIQUETTE

Email can be a highly effective tool for workplace communications. But when employees use email improperly it serves as a serious source of frustration for their co-workers and customers.

Here are seven email etiquette tips to maximize the effectiveness of your messages:

1. Use an opening and closing salutation with each message. Example:

    Hi Joan, Here is the information I promised.
    Thanks, Deb

2. Get directly to the point. The "meat" of the message should be clearly communicated in the first two lines.

3. When there is a considerable amount of information, organize it into readable material by using bullets and a space between each of the points.

4. Do not use jargon, buzz words or acronyms, unless you are absolutely certain that every recipient of your email will understand their meanings.

5. Never, ever make inflammatory or critical statements about another individual in an email message.

6. Cute symbols, such as smiley faces, tend to annoy most email readers. (They are acceptable on hand-written inter-office notes).

7. Limit the number of email messages you send. Never use email to avoid face-to-face or telephone conversations with your customers and co-workers.

TAMING THE EMAIL BEAST

Do you feel like email is devouring your time? You're not alone. According to research, the average U.S. worker spends up to four hours each day sending and receiving email. This can create a time management problem for employees and managers.

If email is dominating your day, it's also damaging your productivity. You need to tame the beast and take back your time. Are you lured to your computer to check email every time it arrives in your inbox? If so, you're wasting valuable time. These interruptions impair productivity. Now is the time for you to develop an email management system.

Here's the system that works for me:

♦ Mute your computer speakers so that you don't hear the alert every time a message arrives. Don't be a "slave" to your computer tones. If you can hear your messages arriving, they will interrupt your thoughts, conversations and creativity.

♦ Don't leave your email program open. It's too tempting to glance at it every time a message is received. Even if you're not reading the messages, they are causing you stress and disrupting your concentration.

♦ Develop a consistent schedule for email "quick checks." Try to schedule no more than four email checks per day. Choose the times that work best for you. During these email "quick checks," only respond to those matters that require immediate attention.

♦ For example: you can check your messages one hour after you get to work. Very few important messages will have arrived between the time you left yesterday and the time you arrive today. Waiting one hour will allow your co-workers and customers to get their first messages of the day to you, and still give you plenty of time to respond. Start your day by working on those high priority projects that are awaiting completion.

- ♦ Your second email check can occur right before lunchtime. Schedule one around mid-afternoon, and your last check just before you leave for the day.

- ♦ Manage your email efficiently. In order to work effectively and present a professional image, it is critical to keep your work area organized and free of clutter. View your email inbox as an extension of your workspace. Schedule 15-30 minutes twice each day to manage the messages that are cluttering your inbox.

The Loyalty Leader®'s 5 Rs of Email Management:

The goal of this management program is to reduce the number of emails you keep in your inbox so that you are not constantly reviewing the same material. Just like regular mail and documents, it's important to develop a "one-touch" system whenever possible.

Review

Read your messages and prioritize them by importance. If you have allowed your inbox to become excessively full, you may need to use a pad of paper to list the messages by sender and subject in the order of importance. Set up three columns, "Urgent," "Need Additional Info" and "Filing."

Respond

Open the item and respond immediately to those messages that require action on your part. If you are not prepared to provide all of the information the sender has requested, respond with a promised date and time of delivery. Keep your promise.

Remove

Immediately delete any item that is a duplicate of another message, outdated or irrelevant information, inappropriate content such as SPAM and chain letters, or a message that does not require any response. If you're uncomfortable about deleting the message, store it in an appropriate folder.

Record

For email messages that require further follow-up or need to be retained as business records, set up a system of folders for filing those messages. It's easy to do in Microsoft Outlook. Simply click on the "Organize" button and create folders that make sense for organizing your material. For example: folder labels can include: "Due Monday," "Requests from the Boss," "Strategic Plan," "Upcoming Meetings," etc.

Reorganize

If email is an absolutely essential form of communication, necessary for effectively doing your job (think this through very carefully), make a commitment to review your folders once a month to delete unnecessary messages or move the items to new folders. Keep your inbox as empty as possible and organize your folders in a way that makes information easy to access. By doing so, you too can tame the email beast.

INCREASE YOUR CUSTOMER SERVICE TELEPHONE POWER

The Council of Better Business Bureaus has seen a steady increase in the number of customer service complaints, which topped 2.8 million last year.

About 85 percent of customer-to-company contact takes place over the phone. Among the businesses consumers are least happy with are banks, department stores, airlines, hospitals, hotels and phone companies.

A few smart firms have realized that there's a big pay-off for doing it right. So what are they doing differently?

Amazon.com is committed to the reality that loyalty does start at the top and CEO Jeff Bezos continues to answer email from customers every week. Amazon.com reps have the authority to spend as long as it takes to solve a customer's problems—and permission to go up the ladder all the way to the CEO if necessary.

FedEx views customer service as everyone's job, from the carrier who delivers the package to the customer service reps who answer the calls.

Land's End answers 90 percent of its calls in 20 seconds or less. And the average customer service rep has been with the company seven to nine years. If customers want to call to just chat about the weather, the reps chat with them and that's just fine with upper management.

Verizon Communications employees receive up to 12 weeks of initial customer service training. When customers call or write in to thank Verizon for great service, the entire customer service team is rewarded with candy bars or other incentives.

The best businesses strive for what's known as "one-and-done service." "That means you call one number, talk to one person and get your questions answered," says Jon Anton, director of benchmark research at Purdue University Center for Customer-Driven Quality. The gold standard also includes 24/7 access via Internet, email and phone, but it's estimated that only 20 percent of the 12 million U.S. companies are meeting that standard.

Here are four things your company can do to power up its telephone customer service:

1. Stay current with computer technology and software that makes it easy for employees to access customer information and transfer calls and account details to another person.

2.   Provide better training and give employees the freedom to handle customer service issues in a way that's best for the customer, not always according to the company rule book.

3.   Don't cut corners when hiring customer service staff. Building a lifetime relationship with your customers is your best investment in the future success of the company.

4.   Let callers know just how long their wait times will be so they know what to expect.

TUNE UP YOUR TELEPHONE SKILLS

How do you sound to your customers and co-workers? Many transactions with your internal and external customers are done completely by phone without any personal contact.

First impressions are lasting impressions. That's why every telephone conversation counts. The impression you make on an internal or external customer is entirely dependent upon the way you sound. A single phone conversation can determine whether or not a customer will continue to do business with your company. The way you handle each call reflects on your department, your company and, most importantly, on you.

Having an awareness of what you sound like is just the first step in improving your telephone skills. When you know what to listen for, you find that you can correct verbal habits and mannerisms that may create barriers between you and your customers.

Here are 5 easy tips for your telephone voice:

1.   Smile! Your speech is automatically energized and will convey a pleasant and cooperative attitude.

2.   Good posture will inject more enthusiasm in your voice. Sitting up straight will make you sound better.

3.   Be an attentive listener so you can understand your customer's needs.

4. Avoid being distracted by others. Stay focused on your call.

5. Be courteous at all times, and remain professional.

The way you take phone messages for your co-workers or boss reflects on you and your organization.

HOW TO TAKE PROPER PHONE MESSAGES

The way in which you take phone messages for your co-workers or boss reflects on you and your organization. It can also impact the quality of customer service that your co-worker is able to deliver.

Here are seven message-taking tips to make you look good:

1. Explain that the person to whom they wish to speak is unavailable. (It is not necessary to give the caller details).

2. Ask if you or anyone else can help them.

3. Don't promise any activity on the part of the person for whom you are taking the message.

4. Spell the caller's name correctly and include the area code, phone number, plus the date and time of the call. Repeat all of the information and ask the caller to verify that it is accurate.

5. Find out how soon the caller needs the call returned and what is the most convenient time to reach them.

6. Write the purpose of the call and the expectations of the caller on the message.

7. Keep your note brief and deliver it as soon as possible.

WEAK WORDS SPELL TROUBLE ON THE TELEPHONE

If the majority of your customer communications take place by telephone, then consider this as your new job title, "Director of First Impressions." It's important for you to take complete ownership of your phone etiquette. It not only reflects on you, but also can shape the caller's impression of your whole department. And impacts the organization's bottom line.

Think about the times when you've dreaded calling another department or co-worker. Or the times you've called an organization only to be left with the feeling that the major concern the person on the other end of the line had for your call was to find a way to pass the problem on to someone else. You can probably recollect phone calls that left you feeling frustrated or irritated. These situations probably occurred because individuals using weak words or expressions greeted you.

The language you use can make or break each call. There are certain words and phrases that are so weak or offensive, they can quickly turn off your caller and spell trouble for you. Here are examples of weak words and expressions to avoid:

♦ **"You should have..." or "Why didn't you...?" or "You have to...?"**
   These expressions sound like you're blaming the caller rather than focusing on the source of the problem. They also tell your caller that you're not willing to take ownership. This may cause the caller to think you're being condescending and they will often get defensive. Rather than pointing out your caller's mistakes, focus on what you can do to fix the problem by saying, "Thank you for

bringing this to my attention. Let's see what I can do to help you get this resolved."

◆ **"I will try to get that to you."**
The word to look out for here is "try." "Try" is a weak word that gives your caller the feeling that his or her request is not going to be handled well. It can also be interpreted as a lack of competency and professionalism. Be positive and prepared to commit by saying, "I will get that done for you." Make sure, however, that you have the resources and authority to follow through on your promise.

◆ **"Hang on."**
This expression can make you sound flip or too casual. The more appropriate response is to ask, "May I put you on hold?"

◆ **"Yeah or Yup."**
Remember, you are a professional. The correct word to use is "yes." You will sound crisper, more educated and actually friendlier.

◆ **"Uhh, umm, ya' know."**
These are filler words that are often interpreted by customers as a lack of knowledge or education. If you are not sure how to answer your caller's question, say, "That's a great question. May I put you on hold while I find the answer?"

Even small lapses in proper phone etiquette can leave your customers questioning the professionalism of your organization. If they occur frequently, your customers may consider taking their business elsewhere. Learning proper business telephone etiquette is not difficult. You begin by identifying those words and phrases that are guaranteed to annoy customers and learning to replace them with words that build trust and rapport.

HOW TO DELIVER SEAMLESS SERVICE

When customers contact your organization, they deserve to receive exceptional service without having to navigate through an obstacle course. Obstacles may include a complicated phone system, the inability to talk to a "live" person, long "hold" times, or being transferred to other departments where they are asked to repeat their request multiple times.

Seamless service requires that every employee throughout the organization operates as part of a team in order to meet the needs of the customer. It's a way of streamlining service requests without the customers feeling the pain. When this occurs, customers feel more in control of their own destiny. As a result, your customers feel certain that they are valued.

Take this quick quiz to see how well you understand the difference between adequate service and seamless service. Select the response that best demonstrates seamless service in each of these scenarios:

A.   You receive a phone call from a customer who has a service request. You quickly realize that you are not the person who is equipped to help this particular customer. In a warm, friendly voice you say to the customer:

> 1.   *"I'm sorry, we don't handle that in this department, I'll transfer you to our purchasing department. Please hold while I transfer your call."*
>
> 2.   *"The employees in our purchasing department would best be able to handle your request. May I put you on hold while I contact someone in that department to explain your situation?"*

If you selected #2, you were correct. One goal of seamless service is to do everything you can to prevent your customers from having to tell their story over and over. Every time your customers need to repeat their requests, loyalty goes down.

B.   You need to transfer a call to another department and you want to communicate in a way that will be least offensive to your customer. You say to your customer:

> *1.   "The employees in our customer service department will be happy to help you with your request. May I transfer your call to that department?"*
>
> *2.   "Just a moment while I transfer you to the customer service department."*

If you selected #1, you were correct. It is always better to "ask" your customers for permission rather than "telling" them you are going to transfer their calls.

Hot tip! If you ask your customers, "May I transfer your call?" you need to wait for their answer before proceeding.

C.   You know that after you transfer your customer's call, he or she will be placed into another queue and will have to wait before an employee will answer. You say to your customer:

> *1.   "You may be on hold again once I transfer your call."*
>
> *2.   "Due to the high volume of calls coming into that area today, you can expect to be on hold for up to five minutes after I transfer your call. Is this acceptable or would you prefer that I have someone from that department call you back?"*

If you selected #2, you were correct. When a customer is going to be inconvenienced in any way, it is important to explain the reason: "Due to the high volume of calls..." Also, recognize that time is your customer's most precious commodity. Most customers do not mind being placed on hold when they know how long they are expected to wait. But if you really want to build loyalty, help them to control their destiny by offering the option of not waiting and receiving a return phone call instead.

Seamless service may sound like it takes more time and effort than satisfactory service, but in the long run it actually saves time for both you and your customer. Everyone who works in your organization is part of the same team. When your customers perceive that service is a team approach, where every employee takes complete ownership of his or her role in the customer service chain, loyalty is sure to follow.

CELL PHONE ETIQUETTE: BLUNDERS AND BASICS

A little cell phone ringing in the back of the room was all it took to cause Mike Sherman, former coach of the Green Bay Packers, to walk out in the middle of a press conference.

"It's a total lack of respect for each other. Forget me. You don't have to respect me, but respect each other," said Sherman.

The media reported that some thought Sherman over-reacted, but the majority of people polled supported his actions because they're irritated with the lack of courtesy by cell phone users.

Cell phone abuse is creeping into the workplace. A senior executive of a large company interrupted a training seminar I was presenting for his employees. He said, "I just need about five minutes to tell the employees how much they're appreciated."

I'm a big supporter of employee recognition so I stepped aside and gave him the platform.

He began his speech by telling the employees how important they are and thanking them for a job well done. After a few minutes, the cell phone in his pocket buzzed. He stopped talking, pulled it out and checked the display. When he returned it to his pocket, he continued his speech. A moment later, out came his phone. He checked the display and placed it back in the pocket. Then he looked up at the group and said, "Now, let's see. Where was I?"

He repeated this ritual with his cell phone three more times during his presentation. I looked around the room each time it occurred. The body language of the employees told the whole story. Several were angrily whispering to one another. Many were rolling their eyes and folding their arms in exasperation. Some wore expressions of stunned disbelief that this executive would choose to behave so rudely.

His five-minute speech turned into a 25-minute exercise in frustration for the whole team. His actions sent a much louder message than his words. Instead of recognizing the employees, he communicated that the phone calls he was receiving were of greater value than the time he was spending with them.

There are more and more complaints emerging about cell phones in the workplace. The abuses are numerous: the executive who takes a call in the middle of a meeting; the phones left on in cubicles that blast loud, annoying ring tones; the seminar leader who interrupts his speech to take a call on his cell; the co-worker who discusses vacation plans with her husband.

Unlike many new technologies, even the people who love cell phones consider them a nuisance. A recent University of Michigan poll of 752 adults found that 6 of 10 users found public cell phone use "a major irritation."

In 2006, the Society for Human Resource Management (SHRM) surveyed 379 human resource professionals and found that 40 percent of their companies had formal policies governing cell phone use at work.

If cell phone use and abuse is creating problems in your workplace, it's time to create and implement a set of guidelines for cell phone etiquette. These guidelines need to begin with the premise that employees are paid to work, not take personal calls.

Studies reveal that the busier an individual is the less likely he or she is to take time and be interrupted by personal phone calls. Conversely, individuals with time on their hands fill the day with personal calls.

Here are some guidelines to help you get started:

♦   Company-issued cell phones are the property of the business. Prohibiting the use of company-owned cell phones for personal calls is permissible.

♦   Limit personal cell phone use to lunch hours and breaks.

♦   Personal cell phones must be turned off and stored during business hours.

♦   Do not allow ring tones of any kind.

♦   Employees who cannot be reached on a direct company line may use their phones in case of an emergency only.

♦   Do not allow cell phone use within 30 feet of another employee, even on breaks.

Cell phones are here to stay and because they are so intrusive, their use needs to be managed in the workplace. Lack of cell phone courtesy is creating a set of problems similar to the problems caused by email. The best way to develop cell phone etiquette guidelines is to look in the mirror and ask yourself, "Am I guilty of committing the same cell phone sins that drive me crazy when others do them?"

WATCH YOUR LANGUAGE!

The quality of everyday language used in business is on the decline. We are often unaware of the impact that our words have on our customers. When we use language that is negative or abrupt, we create communication barriers that will frustrate and offend people. Negative language can quickly destroy even the strongest business relationships.

Below are four types of phrases that most people find irritating and some guidelines for changing them from negative to positive phrases:

Giving orders to your customers

Rather than:

> "You have to..."
> "You must..."

Use:

> "If you will _____, then I can..."
> "In order to _____, we need..."

Focusing on what you can't do instead of what you can do

Rather than:

> "I can't do that..."
> "We don't do that..."
> "You can't..."

Use:

> "Here is what I can do for you."
> "Let's see what we can do."
> "Here is what you can do..."

Criticizing or "blaming" your customers

Rather than:

> "You should have..."
> "You never..."
> "You failed to..."

Use:

> "Here's how we can resolve this..."
> "Often..."
> "We did not receive..."

Appearing unknowledgeable or unwilling to help

Rather than:

> "I don't know."

Use:

> "I'll be happy to check on that for you."
> "Let me find out for you."

The ability to recognize and change your negative language into positive phrases will provide you with excellent tools to build lasting customer relationships. It takes integrity and practice to master positive communication skills. But when you do, you will see immediate results in the delighted responses of your co-workers and customers.

MUSIC TO YOUR CUSTOMER'S EARS

Upon returning home after a busy, stressful day, I heard this message on my answering machine:

> "Hi. This is Noelle from Visual Image Photography. I heard that you're the new chairperson responsible for coordinating the soccer club picture night in your community. I'm here to make that job assignment so easy for you. It'll be like a walk in the park!"

Noelle's words were music to my ears. Her message made me smile and it was exactly what I needed to hear. Think about the times you've regretted volunteering to do a task that seemed daunting. Like me, you probably feared that you had committed to something that was going to involve a great deal of time and work.

Your customers often feel the same way. A customer request can be as simple as ordering a hamburger, or as complicated as buying a home. What your customer requests is not nearly as important as how you respond.

When a customer needs your help, the very tone and words you use to respond to their request will make all the difference in the world. Within seconds, your response will shape your customer's perception of you and the company for which you work.

Here are five tips to show your customer you care:

♦ Listen attentively to what your customer is saying. Don't fake it by just acting interested. It's a compliment to your customers when they know they have your undivided attention. You'll also pick up on important details about their interests or concerns.

♦ Smile and use inflection in your voice to demonstrate your enthusiasm.

- Commit to action: "I will personally take care of this for you."

- Respond courteously and patiently to questions. Encourage more questions.

- Replace superficial statements with heartfelt statements that reflect your customer's interests: "Enjoy your afternoon at the zoo with your son." This will be far more appreciated than, "Thank you. Have a nice day."

BE CAREFUL WITH YOUR COMPLIMENTS

I recently ran into a former client of mine. I hadn't seen her in four years. After our initial greeting, she backed off, looked me over and said, "Oh my gosh, you've lost like, a billion pounds!"

The truth was, I had lost about 26 pounds since the last time we worked together. No question about it, I was two sizes larger then, but I had never really thought of myself as huge—until that moment. When we returned home, I pulled out photos of myself from that time period and saw myself in a different way.

The woman is very nice and I've always respected her. I choose to believe that she intended her comment to be a compliment, but it came out as a backhanded compliment. According to Wikipedia, a backhanded compliment or left-handed compliment is an insult disguised as a compliment. It is generally used to belittle or condescend. Often one uses a backhanded compliment when one wants to insult someone in a subtle way.

In business, compliments can go a long way toward building loyalty. Your customers and co-workers want to feel special. The more you acknowledge them in positive ways, the more they will want to develop a positive working relationship with you. But the compliments must be sincere.

You can build loyalty when you celebrate your co-workers' successes with sincere compliments. When you do compliment an employee's specific performance, don't follow up with criticism. For example, "You did a great job on that event Kathy, much better than last time."

Your customers and co-workers want to feel special. Be generous with your compliments and careful about their meanings. Don't compliment someone unless you really mean it. And never throw a dig in at the end, such as, "Great haircut. It really slims your face."

Here are some tips for offering compliments:

Offer a compliment only when you mean it.

I had a former boss who we called "Hi-how-are-ya-Harry." He would walk through the building saying to everybody, "Hi, how are ya?" But he would never wait for anyone's answer. One day, he said to me, "Deb, you're the best!" It made my day. I even went home and told my husband, "Harry told me I'm the best!"

The next day, at an all-staff meeting, I watched Harry as he approached three different employees and said, "You're the best!" That's when I realized it was just flattery, empty words that carried no meaning at all.

Be timely with your compliments.

Give a compliment immediately after the event that prompts your praise. There are plenty of opportunities to compliment your customers and co-workers, even on the phone. When someone has been patient during a long transaction, you can say, "Thank you for waiting. It was kind of you to be so patient."

Don't use compliments to manipulate others.

When you tell a co-worker how much you admire his or her willingness to help others, pleasure will turn to annoyance when you add, "By the way, could you cover for me tomorrow afternoon so I can take my son to the dentist?"

Issue compliments in moderation.

If you compliment every customer and every co-worker too frequently, you may earn the reputation of my former boss. Give a compliment only when the situation or person warrants it. On the other hand, you can be on the lookout for opportunities to compliment someone. You can even offer a compliment when a customer complains: "Thank you so much for giving me a little more of your valuable time today so that I could get this resolved."

Be specific about the reason for the compliment.

Avoid making over-generalized or blanket compliments. If a customer enters your place of business with a child, acknowledge the child and make your compliment as specific as possible: "Is this your daughter? I love her curly hair."

When you earn a reputation as someone who takes time to recognize and compliment positive things about others, your customers will choose to do business with you because you make them feel special. Your co-workers will be more supportive of you and will enjoy having you on their team.

HONESTY STARTS WITH THE SMALL STUFF

> *Our lives improve only when we take chances—and the first and most difficult risk we can take is to be honest with ourselves.'*
> — Walter Anderson

Kevin started out in a middle management position at his company. Although this salary was modest, he worked hard and diligently supported his boss on a variety of projects as the business grew.

He was promoted to a senior management position and the CEO took notice of Kevin's dedication and excellent work. He decided to promote Kevin to assistant vice president and the two began working together very closely.

One day the phone rang in the conference room where they were meeting. Kevin answered and said, "Just a moment."

He covered the mouthpiece, then turned to the CEO and said, "It's Kurt in accounting. He needs some information regarding the upcoming merger."

The CEO shook his head and whispered, "Tell him I'm not here."

Kevin handed the phone to the CEO and said, "You tell him."

When the CEO had completed the call, he said angrily, "Why didn't you tell him I wasn't here?"

Kevin replied, "If I can lie to Kurt, I can lie to you. And if you can't trust me, I'm no good for you or this company."

How many times have you been faced with decisions where you could just "bend" the truth a little? You may be frustrated with the behavior of a co-worker, but rather than telling her directly, you talk about the problem with others.

Your boss asks you to tell callers that he's in a meeting when he's actually in his office completing a report. Your favorite customer asks you to make an exception for her even when you know it's against company policy.

There are many reasons you can list to justify your decisions:

- ♦ "I don't want to hurt that person's feelings by telling the truth."

- ♦ "I don't want that person to become angry with me."

- ♦ "I don't want to make waves."

- ♦ "I do what my boss tells me to do because I'm afraid I might lose my job or miss the chance to get promoted."

- ♦ "I want to help my customer and it won't hurt the company if I bend this rule without permission to do so."

Employees and customers are craving honesty. When my husband, Larry, called his doctor to schedule a medical test, he requested a late afternoon appointment. He was told that only mornings were available.

When Larry questioned the receptionist about the reason, he was delighted by her refreshingly honest response, "Well, to be frank with you, our doctors enjoy golfing and want to play as much as they can while the weather is still nice. We're not allowed to book afternoon appointments."

Here are some tips to help you to focus on honesty, even in tough situations:

- ♦ Take a few deep breaths before speaking. This will help you to become emotionally neutral about the person or situation.

- ♦ State the issue as specifically as possible. Keep your tone even and pleasant.

- ◆   Choose not to blame another person. Just stick to the simple facts and repeat them if necessary.

- ◆   Avoid "over-explaining" the reasons for your decision. When you choose to be honest, you do not need to justify your decision to anyone.

Honesty is something that needs to be practiced. And the best way to learn is by choosing the truth, even in small, seemingly trivial situations. Sometimes we react defensively to a situation or request and tell a little white lie when it would be just as easy to tell the truth.

For example, my son's friend was invited by his soccer coach to be a substitute player on the team in an upcoming tournament. Both kids were excited about the opportunity to play together on the same team.

A few days before the tournament, I received an email from the coach. She wrote that my son's friend may not be able to play after all. His birthday missed the cut-off date for eligibility by seven days. She wondered if she should just list a different birth date on the registration form so he could still play.

I'll admit, I hesitated for a minute and thought, "What's the harm? It's only a few days difference and then the kids won't be disappointed."

But I caught myself and replied with a message telling her that I wasn't comfortable listing a false birth date on the registration form. The coach agreed. Ironically, the league let the friend play anyway, so everything turned out the way we had hoped.

Choosing to go the honest route not only made me feel good, it also cemented a relationship of mutual respect between the coach and me.

"PLEASE ACCEPT OUR SINCERE SYMPATHY"

My father passed away in 1994. Just recently, I received a very nice form letter from a customer service representative of an insurance company that began, "On behalf of our company, I extend our sincere sympathy on the loss of your father."

The letter went on to explain that dad had a small life insurance policy that had never been claimed by his children because we hadn't known it existed. The letter surprised me so that I called my brothers and sister to see if they knew anything about this. They didn't. I was concerned that it might be a scam because it was asking for our social security numbers.

Enter Edward. An agent's name and phone number was included at the end of the letter. I called him and discovered that that he had never heard of my father but said he'd look into the matter for our family. Fifteen minutes later, Edward called back and said, "I called our company headquarters and this is legitimate. It looks like your dad took out a small policy back in 1946 and the company just recently tracked you down."

It turns out that the agent lives in an assisted living center. He's been selling life insurance for 50 years and had begun ten years after my dad bought the policy. He had me fax a copy of the letter to him that he then collected from the nurses' station where he lives. He made several calls on my behalf and always got back to me within minutes of getting the answers.

I thanked him over and over for taking the time to help us cut through the red tape and get the matter straightened out. All he asked for in return was a couple of pleasant, chatty conversations to help fill his lonely hours. I told him that if he wasn't semi-retired, I'd refer everyone I knew who need life insurance.

Thanks to Edward's willingness to go the extra mile, my siblings and I received our benefit checks four days after he helped us straighten out the claim. Inserted with the check was another letter, which began, "We're sorry for your recent loss. We know this can be a difficult time for you and have enclosed a list of resources to help you cope with the grief..."

Loyalty Leader® Quick Tip: Take time to read form letters before you send them to make sure the message fits the circumstances!

SELF-ASSESSMENT

ARE YOU A POSITIVE OR NEGATIVE LISTENER?

An important aspect of communicating well is listening well. Take this quiz to evaluate your listening skills. A positive listener makes the person who is speaking feel valued by demonstrating interest in a sincere way.

♦ **Am I a positive listener?**

1. I give encouragement to the person who is speaking and reassure him or her that I'm interested.
   True   False

2. I say to the speaker, "Tell me more about that."
   True   False

3. I echo or paraphrase important messages to let the speaker know I'm actively listening.
   True   False

4. I ask specific questions and listen for clues as to what the speaker's deeper interest in the subject may be.
   True   False

♦ **Am I a negative listener?**

1. I say to the speaker, "I know just what you mean."
   True   False

2. I glance away from the speaker while he or she is talking.
   True   False

3. I frequently turn the conversation back to myself to share my opinions or ideas.
   True   False

4. I often think I know the other person's point of view before he or she has shared it.
   True   False

9 WAYS TO BECOME A BETTER LISTENER

The challenges of a fast-paced world make many people poor listeners. Effective listening plays a critical role in business. The most successful people I know are people with solid listening skills. Improving your ability to listen will help you to earn respect, advance your career and generally improve all of your relationships.

Here are 9 ways to become a better listener:

1. Evaluate your listening skills by paying attention to how you currently interact with others.

2. Avoid distractions so you can concentrate on what the other person is saying.

3. Send nonverbal messages through eye contact and body language to indicate that you have heard what is being said.

4. Don't be too quick to judge or offer an opinion even when you agree with the other person.

5. Practice reflective listening by paraphrasing what the other person has said.

6. Ask good, open-ended questions to clarify your understanding and to show your interest.

7. Learn to distinguish when commenting is worth it and when it's not.

8. Encourage the other person by exhibiting sincere enthusiasm and respect.

9. Set aside your ego to focus less on you and more on the other person.

CHAPTER 6

CUSTOMER SERVICE
AND SALES

In the world of Internet Customer Service, it's important to remember your competitor is only one mouse click away.

— Doug Warner

Although your customers won't love you if you give bad service, your competitors will.

— Kate Zabriskie

PUT YOUR HOUSE IN ORDER
TO SUPPORT MARKETING

The word "marketing" conjures up images of a written plan, direct mail and slick brochures. But there's another side of marketing that's far more important than the most compelling advertising campaign. It is the unspoken messages that your organization sends out every day to existing and potential customers. This type of marketing speaks more loudly and can do greater good or damage than any paid advertising message.

When we invite guests into our home, we clean the house, prepare good food, shower and dress nicely and try to put our best foot forward. In other words, we "put our house in order."

We need to do the same things with our businesses. The first and most critical step in developing a marketing plan is "putting your house in order." Identifying and eliminating problems within your organization that create a negative marketing image can accomplish this. These can include everything from gossiping employees to peeling paint. When you have internal problems, they can seriously damage your image with your external customers. They need to be fixed before you embark on a marketing campaign.

Here are examples of negative marketing activities that I've personally observed:

- ◆ While sitting in my car at the bank drive-through, two employees came out the back door, slouched against the wall and lit up cigarettes. Then they started loudly complaining about their boss and a co-worker. Their tirade went on for about ten minutes and included obscenities. I had to close my car window so my son wouldn't be able to hear their vulgar language.

- ◆ As I paid my money to the clerk at a fast-food drive-through window, I noticed that he had excessively long fingernails that were ragged and filthy. His nails were so long that he actually scratched my hand as he handed back my change. I lost my appetite.

- ◆ I shop at a family-owned grocery store in an upscale neighborhood because they are known for their excellent quality meat and produce. The quality is high but so are the prices and they attract a wealthy clientele that is eighty percent female. So I was shocked when I used their only restroom. The floor, sink, soap dispenser and toilet were dirty. The walls had peeling paint, the wastebasket was over-flowing and the paper towel dispenser was empty. It sure made me think twice about the quality of the establishment.

♦ I asked the clerk at a jewelry store to give me the store's website address so I could do some additional shopping from the comfort of my home. She told me, "I don't know if we even have a website. And if we do, I sure don't know the address." I've made no further purchases there.

♦ A local grocery store ran an ad in the Sunday newspaper to promote a special on gallons of milk. The store did not have enough of the advertised brand on hand and sold out of the product before noon. Although the store offered "rain checks" after running out, a lot of customers were annoyed. This did more damage to the store's image than if the special had not been offered in the first place.

Every one of those scenarios sent a powerful negative marketing message to the people who keep these organizations in business—their customers. It is absolutely pointless to develop a marketing campaign designed to bring in new business if customers are going to be met with:

♦ Poorly trained employees

♦ Negative attitudes

♦ Employees who are inappropriately dressed or have poor hygiene

♦ An unkempt or unattractive environment

♦ An inadequate supply of advertised products or services

Before you design a marketing plan and invest money in advertising campaigns to bring new customers through your doors, you must first address the issues that are harming relationships with your existing customers. In other words, "put your house in order" before you invite new guests!

SALES AND SERVICE AREN'T SEPARATE DEPARTMENTS

The most important aspect of sales is getting the customer. The most important aspect of service is *keeping* the customer. Both impact the bottom line. Customer trust is essential to repeat business. But trust will erode if your customers hear one message from a sales representative and a different message from a customer service representative.

As a salesperson, you need to have a good reputation not only with your customers, but also with everyone on the customer service team. This means that you need to communicate frequently and openly with customer service reps. This is especially important when promises have been made to the customer.

Customer service representatives need to give ongoing feedback to members of the sales team. They can alert sales reps about the types of situations that increase customer complaints or enhance customer satisfaction. Employees in both departments experience the highest levels of customer contact in the company. The quality of communication between the two departments can significantly increase or decrease customer loyalty.

There is nothing worse for a sales rep than a customer service rep denying a request that had been promised to the customer. There is nothing worse for a customer service rep than a customer making a demand that requires breaking the rules, only to find out that a sales rep assured him or her they could do it.

There is nothing worse for the customer than to be caught in the middle between the promises of sales and the rules of customer service. Customer loyalty increases when employees in the sales and service departments present a united front to customers. Schedule a monthly meeting to open the lines of communication between sales and service. If it's not possible for everyone to attend, assign a liaison from each department who can report on behalf of his or her team.

Sales topics should include special promotions being offered by sales, new customer profiles and any other sales activities that may impact the service department. Customer service topics should include frequent requests, trends in complaints and new policies that may impact sales.

Customer retention is the lifeblood of any successful sales operation. It takes trust, and every salesperson needs to build trust with all employees in the organization if they want to keep their existing customers. Most importantly, open communication between the sales and customer service teams will give everyone the opportunity to do what's best for the customer without compromising integrity.

CREATING CUSTOMER BUZZ

When people say great things about your company your business is sure to grow. Creating a "buzz" is more powerful than advertising because it is based on trust. We're more likely to believe what our friends and co-workers tell us.

Here are some tips to get your customers buzzing about your business:

- ◆ Avoid "bad buzz"
    - • Give people something positive to talk about. When problems occur, fix them fast.

- Put customer testimonials on your website.
- Look for ways to surprise and delight your customers through unexpected service.

◆ Get people talking

- Send free samples of new products or sponsor a contest where customers can win free product. Trivial Pursuit was an unknown game until its producer's public relations department began sending copies to the celebrities mentioned in the game.

◆ Create excitement.

- Be creative. For example, when a customer is awaiting the shipment of a new sofa, you can send her a card with a picture of the sofa in it. Include a handwritten note that says "I can't wait to settle into my new home and meet the family."
- Send a "Welcome Home" basket to banking customers who have just closed on their new home mortgage.

◆ Create an internal buzz.

- Schedule employee meetings with individual departments in buzz brainstorming. This sparks enthusiasm for your products and services because every employee shares new ideas on how to create the buzz.

Keep in mind that you can't rely solely on buzz. Word-of-mouth is powerful but it often spreads slowly. You'll need traditional marketing and advertising to fan the flames started by the spark of a buzz.

YOU'RE IN SALES...
NO MATTER WHAT YOUR TITLE

If I ask you right now whether or not you are in sales, chances are you would say, "No, I'm in accounts payable or customer service or marketing." You might even say, "I'm the CEO."

No matter what your job is, you are in sales. Every time you interact with a customer, you are selling your professional credibility, the company's products or services and the company's image. So, even if you don't work in the sales department, read on.

When a customer has a bad experience in shipping, in accounting, in technical support or any other department in your company, you can bet that negative word-of-mouth will follow. That word of mouth reduces sales in the same way that customer testimonials increase referrals and sales. You are selling all the time, so it's important for you to recognize what your customers want from you.

Regardless of who your customers are, there are five key actions they want from you:

1.   **To have you spend more time listening than talking**
     Whom do you find more interesting to talk with; the person who rattles on and on sharing his or her wealth of knowledge, or the person who asks you about yourself and then listens to your response?

     Your customers do not call in order to be impressed. They call because they have a need or a problem and believe your company can offer the solution. But before they decide to do business with your company, they are going to decide if they like you and can trust you. Asking your customers intelligent questions and then actively listening to their responses is the best way to build trust and get at the heart of what your customer really needs.

2. **To have things explained in a way they can understand**
    So often, people sell confusion rather than solutions to
    customers. In today's high-tech world, many products and
    services on the market are quite complex. I don't know
    about you, but I'm technically challenged. So when I
    contact technical support to get help with my computers or
    phone system or software, I want to talk to support reps
    who can clearly communicate the solutions.

    Your customers don't want to be insulted by listening to
    jargon and acronyms that are meaningless to anyone who
    doesn't work in that industry. They also don't want to deal
    with a condescending employee who sounds exasperated
    because they're not catching on.

3. **To deal with nice people**
    It's like a breath of fresh air when your customer is greeted
    by a friendly voice answering the telephone or a smile as
    he or she walks through the door. Remember that your
    customers are most likely bumping into negativity every-
    where they go. They deal with traffic jams, long lines in
    stores, frustrations at work, stress at home and more. When
    they pick up the phone to call your company, they want to
    talk to a "nice" person. They need to believe that you are
    someone who genuinely cares about their concerns. They
    want you to sound warm and friendly. They want you to
    treat them like an old friend.

4. **To have their time valued...not wasted**
    Your customers are juggling their schedules to make time
    to contact your company. If they feel their time has been
    wasted, they are far less likely to return. Classic time-
    wasters are placing customers on hold, transferring their
    calls to other departments, not getting their requests right
    the first time and not dealing with knowledgeable employ-
    ees who are empowered to make decisions. Take a look at
    how you're handling your customers' calls and identify the
    situations that waste a customer's time and eliminate those.

5. **To be offered solutions**
    Your customers wouldn't call if they didn't need what your
    company has to offer. Once they get through, they want to
    know that you have the resources and the willingness to do
    everything you can to deliver what they need. This will
    often mean that you need to go the extra mile to explore a
    variety of solutions for them. Or, you will need to help
    them build a relationship with a co-worker who has more
    expertise than you in a given situation.

    In other words, don't cut your customers short with
    responses like, "I don't know," or "We don't do that in this
    department." Instead, commit yourself to being a possibil-
    ity thinker for your customers.

You are impacting your company's sales every time you talk with
a customer. Your goal should be to want your customer to leave
with a strong positive feeling about you and the company. You
can help your customers feel comfortable with the decision to buy
by reinforcing their decision. Show enthusiasm for your products
or services and sincerely thank your customers for choosing your
company. Above all, communicate to your customers that
everyone in the company is part of one big team whose goal it is
to make them happy.

NEVER CRITICIZE THE COMPETITION

Our son was growing so fast that his toes were sticking over the
end of his bed and he barely had room to roll over. It was time to
purchase a larger bed. After visiting numerous furniture stores,
we finally found the perfect bed. Now it came time to buy the
mattress and box spring. The furniture store had a nice selection
and the salesperson was knowledgeable and extremely helpful.

I informed him that we had made our prior mattress purchases from a well-known chain with a reputation for quality. He

listened carefully and agreed that his competitor made excellent mattresses. In fact, he said, "Here are the specifications and prices for our mattresses. The other company has a store just a mile down the road from us. If you have time, why don't you head over there and do a comparison. If you've been happy with them, you may not want to switch." He even wrote out directions to the competitor's site.

We drove over to the other store and were greeted enthusiastically by an aggressive sales manager. I explained that we had purchased mattresses from their company in the past, but I was considering another brand and wanted to do some comparing. He immediately went on the defensive and demanded to know the name of the other store. When I told him, he said, "There's no way their mattresses are as good as ours."

I showed him the specs and pointed out that the other store sells very high-quality furniture and their mattresses also seem to be of very high quality. I also mentioned that their cost was $200 less for a comparable mattress and box spring set.

Again, he said in a defensive tone, "Well, I can knock $200 off the price right now if you don't want our 'free' mattress pad and pillows with your purchase."

"How can you say they're 'free' if the price goes down by $200 when they're not included?" I asked.

This stumped him for a moment, but then, rather than responding to my question, he began to issue warnings about the terrible mistake I would be making if I didn't buy another mattress from his store. I left the store without making the purchase, thinking all the way to my car that perhaps I had made a mistake buying my other mattresses there.

I returned to the furniture store and ordered the new mattress and box spring. I also asked if they would be willing to throw in a mattress pad and pillows at no extra charge. Our sales rep said, "I can't do both, but I'd be happy to make either one of those choices available for you at no cost."

Sold!

Differentiating your company from your competitors is a key part of attracting and retaining customers. But criticizing your competition is the worst way to sell. In today's highly competitive marketplace, your prospective customers have many options available to them. They want to do business with people they know they can trust. People who have their best interests in mind. Criticizing the competition doesn't demonstrate how much you know about your product or your passion for your customers. Rather, you risk the possibility of insulting a customer who may have purchased the very product or service you are condemning.

Focus on your customer's needs. Don't criticize simply because you can. At best, such criticisms will seem gratuitous and, at worst, desperate. Customer service representatives and salespeople who fail to put an emphasis on developing trust and rapport actually do a disservice to their customers and, in effect, create opportunities for their competition. In addition to generating new sales, developing strong relationships will keep competitors at arm's length.

THE HARLEY HOOPLA:
BUILDING CUSTOMER LOYALTY

During August of 2003, more than 300,000 Harley-Davidson® motorcycle owners from all over the world descended on Milwaukee, Wisconsin. They came together to celebrate the company's 100th anniversary. So why all the hoopla? What has Harley done to build this immense base of loyal customers? Let's take a look at five Harley strategies that you can apply to your business to build customer loyalty:

Sell An Experience

Visit the Harley-Davidson® website and you'll see "Experience" as one of the buttons. Offer value to your customers that goes beyond the purchase. Provide resources to help your customers get the most out of your products or services. Harley® offers ride planners, educational materials, customer support, riding classes, tip sheets, and organized tours.

Create An Emotional Connection With Your Customers

Focus on building relationships based on emotional connections with your customers. Find out how they "feel" about doing business with your company. Do they feel reassured, confident or inspired? Do they feel that it's easy or difficult to access service? Successful businesses are sensitive to customer wants and needs. See yourself through your customers' eyes and remember they need more from you than just basic service.

Give Your Customers A Sense Of Belonging

When you buy a Harley, you become a member of a family. Harley-Davidson® established the Harley Owners Group (H.O.G.) in 1983 in response to a desire by Harley riders for an organized way to share their passion and show their pride. Today, there are more than 750,000 members of H.O.G., and it's continuing to grow at a rapid pace. Any organization can create a family atmosphere for its customers.

Send Your Employees To The Customers

Employees at Harley-Davidson® are encouraged to get to know the customers by working at a rally or riding in demo ride. This brings them closer to the customer and helps them to relate to customer needs. Most of the employees become Harley owners or riders.

Bring Your Customers Inside Your Organization

Offer tours of your company. If you don't have a physical location your customers can visit, you may want to give them a virtual tour of the company via a website. Include photos of your customer service team and customers using your products. Keep the site up-to-date with the latest news releases about the company. Invite key customers to your annual meeting and ask them to talk about the good and bad aspects of doing business with the company during the past year. Employees will find this more interesting than listening to someone from marketing say, "Here are the customer satisfaction survey results."

PREMIUM PRICES CALL FOR PREMIUM SERVICE

It goes without saying that when customers are willing to pay premium prices, they expect higher quality products. They also expect premium service and a few perks.

Due to the nature of my business, I often speak at conferences that are held in luxury hotels. This involves an overnight stay where the room rate is over $200 per night. When I spend that kind of money, I assume the hotel will be luxurious. It usually is. I also assume that I will get more for my money than I get from a hotel that costs less than half the price. That's not always the case.

When I arrive, the first thing I see is the huge, beautifully decorated lobby. Check-in goes smoothly as friendly, well-trained desk clerks greet me. It's after I check in that I get frustrated. It seems the higher the price, the more some hotels will "nickel and dime" their guests for every little amenity.

On the way to my room, I stop in the gift shop to purchase a bottle of water. It's half the price of the water provided in the mini-bar in my room.

Once settled in my room, I hook up to the Internet to check my email and learn that I will be charged a daily fee in order to use it. Why is the Internet free at the inexpensive hotels? One would think it could be included as an amenity in a hotel that caters to business travelers who are already paying premium rates.

After I go to bed, I'm awakened several times during the night by the jarring sound of other hotel room doors slamming. I suppose the doors are designed to close quickly for security reasons. But must they slam? Why can't the doors have some kind of a buffer so they close more quietly?

In the morning, I don't always have time to go out for breakfast before my early meetings, so I try to order a muffin and coffee through room service. There's no such thing. I can't order just one muffin; I have to order a basket of four. When the muffins arrive, they're often dry and tasteless. A recent basket of inedible muffins and small pot of coffee ended up costing me over thirty dollars.

There is no question that most luxury hotels are beautiful. But I'll happily trade in some of that beauty for free Internet service, quiet rooms, doors that don't slam and a free muffin with coffee in the morning.

When a guest is already spending a great deal of money just for his or her room, the hotel would go a long way toward building loyalty by including those amenities that make their guests feel valued, rather than charging for services that are included by many smaller chains.

On a recent business trip to a small Midwestern town, I stayed at a Comfort Inn for less than a hundred dollars per night. The hotel was quiet and clean. A warm, friendly clerk greeted me. Internet service was free and I enjoyed a complimentary continental breakfast the next morning before I headed out the door to my meeting. The muffins were moist!

PAMPER YOUR LOYAL CUSTOMERS TO INCREASE SALES

Customer service is selling. It is excellent service that inspires customers to return more often and purchase more products. According to a study by the American Management Association, loyal customers who make repeated purchases because they like the service could yield 65 percent of an organization's sales volume.

Yet, there is a tendency for business owners, customer service representatives and sales representatives to focus their energy in the wrong direction. Things are out of balance when you're spending more time trying to get new customers than you are on building solid relationships with your existing, loyal customers.

Then why do so many people in business take their loyal customers for granted? It's simple: they don't recognize the incredible power this customer base has on their bottom-line results. Sales reps are constantly being told to spend their time prospecting for new customers. While prospecting is important, it's self-defeating if it's done at the expense of building loyalty with current customers.

In many businesses, customer service reps' work is measured on how many calls they complete each day, rather than on the quality of the interactions with their customers. When managers refuse to view service as a marketing strategy, they fail to recognize that a few extra minutes on the phone with a customer could make all the difference in future sales.

Loyal customers are your cheerleaders. They are the people who spread positive word-of-mouth advertising by telling others about your company. They are the customers who will refer new business to you. They will continue to purchase more products and services from you. And, loyal customers are more forgiving when problems do occur.

Exceptional customer service is a powerful selling tool that will give you and your company a long-term competitive advantage. Pamper your loyal customers so they feel recognized and appreciated. Send them an unexpected "thank you" surprise such as a gift card or a book. Call them on a regular basis just to check in, say "hello" and wish them well. Make sure these calls have no strings attached.

They will reward with you with their loyalty, purchases and, most importantly, by telling their friends and colleagues that they trust you enough to give you their business.

STAY IN TOUCH
WITHOUT SMOTHERING YOUR CUSTOMERS

What can you do to keep your customers close without smothering them? Here are some tips for keeping in touch with customers while respecting their boundaries:

◆ **Pay attention to timing.**
When you call a customer, listen carefully to what they're saying between their words. For example, your customer may say, "Thanks for calling." But if their tone is telling you that they are extremely busy or even annoyed by your call, the timing may be off. You need to respect their schedule and keep the call very brief.

◆ **Avoid cookie-cutter letters.**
Nothing will convince your customer that you truly care if you send a form letter that reads "Dear Valued Customer." That type of message will only reinforce their feelings that they are simply regarded as a number rather than a human being with feelings.

- **Don't send mixed signals.**
  Follow-up thank you calls or notes should not contain hidden sales agendas. The "thank you" needs to be sincere and the more personalized the better.

- **Offer value.**
  When you do follow up with a customer, offer value in the form of information, helpful tips, discount coupons or gifts. Forwarding an article that contains information that can benefit your customer's business or personal life will send a message that you paid attention to what's important to them. Customers also enjoy receiving lumpy packages with a small "thank you" gift such as a pen or key chain enclosed.

- **Honor your customers' privacy.**
  If a customer asks you not to call again, honor their request, even if it goes against your company's policy to make three follow-up calls per customer.

LISTEN TO YOUR CUSTOMERS TO CLOSE MORE SALES

Most consumers agree that good listening skills are the most important characteristic of a great salesperson. Yet, many salespeople and customer service reps are so busy talking about their products and services that they don't take time to listen to their customers.

It's been proven that the more questions you ask, the more compelled you will be to listen. When you actively listen, you will learn what is most important to your customer. The net result? You'll be more likely to come up with a solution that will truly meet your customer's needs and experience far greater success in closing the sale.

Due to heavy workloads, short staffing and multi-tasking, many of us have become poor listeners. We pretend we are listening but, in reality, we miss a lot of what is being said to us. We can build much stronger customer and co-worker relationships by becoming better listeners. In order to do this, we need to be able to recognize and overcome our listening barriers.

Seven common barriers to effective listening include:

- Anticipating what the other person will say
- Losing interest in the conversation
- Not paying attention
- Being pre-occupied with other thoughts
- Having preconceived attitudes about the situation or other person
- Jumping to conclusions
- Interrupting

To be effective communicators, we must practice ACTIVE LISTENING. Active listening is hard work. It demands our complete commitment and involves using our eyes, ears, body positioning, brain and heart to understand what the other person is saying. Active listeners constantly search for meaning and request clarification when the meaning is unclear.

Tips for becoming an Active Listener:

- Listen to how things are said as well as to what is said.
- Listen to the words used and voice variation.
- Listen to ideas, opinions and feelings as well as facts.
- Listen to intent, as well as to what is actually expressed by listening between the lines.
- Listen for changes in voice tone or speaking rate.

THANK YOUR CUSTOMERS EVERY CHANCE YOU GET

You can never thank your customers enough. The words are simple enough to say: "Thank you." Then why is it so rare for customers to hear them? What's even more rare is for customers to see those words in writing.

Consumers are starved for recognition. They want to be noticed, valued and appreciated by the people with whom they do business. A primary reason that customers stop doing business with a company is because they don't hear those words, or they're not communicated with sincerity.

Thanking your customers needs to be at the top of your daily "to do" list. When customers receive a handwritten "thank you" note with no strings attached, it is a powerful way to let them know they are truly valued.

It's easy and fun to send notes to your customers. Just set aside 10-15 minutes each day to write three notes. It's just that simple. By the end of the week, you'll have sent 15 "thank you" notes. Now, imagine if every employee in your company took the time to send three "thank you" notes each day. That's a lot of customer appreciation!

Here are four ways that a handwritten "thank you" note builds customer loyalty:

It's unexpected.

Customers simply do not expect to feel appreciated. A simple thank you note will surprise your customers and give them something positive about your company to tell their friends. That's why it's so important to send a "thank you" with no strings attached. Don't enclose your business card or information about a "special offer." Keep the message pure.

It's personal.

Don't use a label for the envelope. A handwritten address and note is more likely to be opened and read by your customer. The fact that you were willing to take the extra time needed to write the message tells your customer that you are sincere.

It's classy.

Handwritten "thank you" notes are viewed as outdated. In the old days, it was considered a disgrace to forget to send a "thank you" note to someone who has done something nice for you. You can probably think of times when your kind deeds or gifts have gone unacknowledged. Every time a customer chooses to do business with you, he or she is giving you a gift. Employees that send handwritten "thank you" notes will stand out from the crowd because it is a classy thing to do.

It's contagious.

The more "thank you" notes you send, the more "seeds" of goodwill you plant. This will benefit you and the company for which you work. Your customers will recognize that you do value them. When customers feel appreciated, they are generally more pleasant and refer more business.

Thank your customers when:

- ◆ They refer a new customer. This one's important because word-of-mouth advertising is what keeps a company healthy.
- ◆ They suggest how you could improve service or other aspects of the business. When your customers feel they've been heard, they automatically feel valued.

- They reach milestone anniversaries as a loyal customer; one year, five years, ten years, etc. A little gift could be included with these "thank you" notes.

- They've been patient with service glitches such as delayed shipping dates, long telephone hold times, website problems, or other issues. This lets your customers know that you recognize the value of their time.

- They've made your day brighter due to their positive attitudes. It's a great way to guarantee more smiles in the future.

- They purchased a product or service based on your recommendation. Your customers have taken some risk when they trust you enough to act on your advice.

- They compliment you, especially in front of another customer or, better yet, your boss. Customers like to hear that their positive comments made a difference.

- They complain and give you the opportunity to resolve the problem. These customers care enough to give your company a second chance.

- They turn down your sales pitch because your product or service wasn't the right fit for them. Just because a customer or prospect says "no" doesn't mean there won't be another opportunity to do business with them in the future.

TOO MUCH CUSTOMER CONTACT

As I was getting a manicure the other day, the receptionist interrupted my nail technician, Angie, and said, "That woman from your Toyota dealer is on the line again. Do you want to take the call?" Angie sighed and instructed her to tell the caller that she was unable to take this type of call while at work.

"What was that about?" I asked.

"That," she said, "is about too much customer service."

Angie went on to explain that she had purchased a new car in January and was satisfied with the buying process. Then the calls started. One week after she picked up her car, a woman from the customer service desk called to see if she was happy with her new car. A week later, she received a second call. They were just checking in to see how everything was going with the vehicle and to make sure that their were no problems.

Since January, Angie had received multiple phone calls from the customer service representative, who basically asked the same questions every time she called. Her customer contact diligence has shifted Angie from being a happy customer to someone who is simply annoyed by too many calls. She told me that the last time she spoke with this representative she told her that she was very happy with the car and there was no need to call again. She also asked her not to call at work anymore. The calls continued.

The same thing happened to me a few years ago. We had our carpets cleaned and a friendly, bubbly woman from the carpet cleaning company began calling to see how we liked their service. The first call was a pleasant surprise. The second call confused me. The third and fourth calls convinced me never to do business with that company again.

There is such a thing as too much customer contact. It's beneficial to follow-up with customers to let them know you love them. But when those calls or letters become a nuisance, it will begin to unravel even the best customer relationships.

BEATING THE PRICING PRESSURE BLUES

The owner of a small business was complaining to me that her sales are down. She told me that her customers are continually asking, "Why don't you have more sales and discounted merchandise at your store?" To try to meet their demands, she held a two-week sale at the end of December where every item in the store was discounted. She offered her customers a 10 percent discount every Friday, and regularly sent emails to her approximately 5,000 customers to notify them of other special sale offers.

This woman was experiencing a bad case of the "pricing pressure blues." She referred to this as the "Wal-Mart mentality," where customers expect everything to always be the lowest price possible. The pressure to keep lowering and defending prices can be draining and demoralizing to business owners, customer service support professionals and sales reps. This creates a downward spiral that causes burnout and frustration. It can even cause a business to close its doors permanently.

There is no such thing as a pricing problem—only a marketing problem. If you are experiencing the pricing pressure blues, it means that you have not differentiated your business sufficiently to make people more willing to buy from you. Differentiation is what makes people want to buy from you rather than buying from the guy down the street. When a business is properly differentiated, it will stand out with the customers and create a situation where customers are willing to pay the higher price. Employees rarely have to defend prices when their company successfully markets the value of its products and the expertise of its staff. Business owners and employees need to focus on differentiating their business from their competitors.

Customers are willing to pay premium prices for products and services when the perceived value is high. For example, take a look at how much people are willing to pay for a cup of coffee at Starbucks. They don't discount their products, they simply make sure each customer feels like they're getting something special for his or her money. How does Starbucks do it? They customize every cup of coffee. The employees learn and use the customers' names. They recognize that a customer's time is valuable, so the employees fly around at top speed to honor that priority. They market their coffee as the "finest," and they invite their customers to stick around and feel at home with fireplaces and wireless Internet services. When a customer walks into Starbucks, they are buying an "experience," not a cup of coffee.

Price is one of the most dangerous ways to differentiate a business. It's a lose-lose proposition because there will always be someone more desperate who will lower their price. Wal-mart does it successfully because it's huge and has access to considerable resources. Rather than fighting the Wal-mart mentality, you need to discover what makes your business, products or services unique.

Find out what matters most to your customers. Is it status, convenience, saving time, your expertise or measurable results? You need to find out how your customers are making their buying decisions for the types of products or services you offer. Ask your current customers these questions:

- ◆ "What did you like about doing business with us?"
- ◆ "What other companies, products or services did you research?"
- ◆ "Why did you decide to buy from us?"
- ◆ "How did we help you to meet your objectives?"
- ◆ "What would you tell others about our company, products or services?"

Business success is all about being different in ways that provide greater value to customers. Every person and business has a WOW factor. In order to differentiate, you need to know your WOW. It's comprised of those unique characteristics that will set you apart from your competition. It gives your customers and prospects something to remember you by. When you discover and learn how to market your WOW, you can add real power to your marketing efforts, boost your sales and overcome the pricing pressure blues.

RETURN YOUR CALLS TO BE SUCCESSFUL

> *"We left a message for you a few days ago but when you didn't return our call, we figured you either weren't available or weren't interested. We needed to make a decision quickly so we hired another speaker."*

When I heard these words, I felt my stomach knot up and I was immediately filled with regret over this missed opportunity. I had no one to blame but myself. Using the excuse of being "too busy," I had procrastinated on returning that call, assuming that the business would still be there when I got around to responding. That was back in 1999.

I only needed to hear those words once to learn my lesson. I immediately made a commitment to respond to calls the same day they come in. Even if I end up leaving a message on the caller's voice mail, at least that individual knows I care enough to return his or her call.

Returning phone calls used to be a common courtesy. Now, busy people claim they don't have the time. I don't buy that excuse. I've found that the most successful, busy people I know are the ones I can rely on to return my call the same day. It's a matter of setting priorities.

If your goal is to attract business or build strong customer relationships, not returning messages or hiding behind closed doors won't win you much success. But, for those times when you're not available, you can employ some reliable methods for managing your calls.

Like me, you probably depend on voice mail to take your messages. Plan to retrieve and respond to calls on a regular basis. If callers know they can count on you to routinely check in, they'll be more comfortable communicating with you in this way. Set aside a specific time of day to return your calls. This will prevent them from snowballing.

Since I'm frequently out of my office conducting seminars, I return all calls that came in during the morning, right before lunch. Then, I return all afternoon calls near the end of the day, preferably before 5 p.m. These two times seem to be great for catching people at their desk, thus preventing endless rounds of phone tag.

It takes far less time to return a phone call than it does to respond to an email message. I can speak much faster than I type. A call is also more personal and lets people know that you value them enough to want to have a conversation with them. Cell phones have made it easy to return calls, even when you're away from your desk.

If you must leave a message, include detailed information. Give the date and time of your call. Answer any questions that the caller asked in his or her original message to you. Let the person know the best time to reach you the next day. Do not leave a laundry list of your entire schedule. It wastes time and will only serve to annoy the person you're calling. If you're concerned about phone tag, invite the other person to call back and let you know the most convenient time to reach him or her. They will usually give you a broad enough time frame to make it easy for you to reach them.

You'll find that by making it easier for people to connect with you, you will strengthen both customer and co-worker relationships. You'll be earning a reputation of professionalism and reliability that will translate into success.

Just recently, I heard these words when I returned a call from a prospective client:

"We called four speakers to inquire about their services for our fall convention. You were the only one who called back the same day. You're hired!"

SWEEPING CUSTOMERS OFF THEIR FEET

When you sweep the stairs, you start at the top.
— German proverb

It's easy to drive right by a little store called "Mr. Vak" in Milwaukee, Wisconsin. The shop is tucked between two other businesses and there's nothing flashy about the display window. When you look in, you'll see, well, vacuum cleaners

I was in the market for a new vacuum cleaner and had been shopping for one at large department and electronics stores. I was getting very frustrated by the lack of knowledge exhibited by the employees who were the so-called "vacuum experts" in these various stores. They were unable to answer my questions about features and differences between models.

Then I discovered Mr. Vak. A young man named Dmitriy owns the store. All he does is sell and service vacuum cleaners. Step inside and you'll experience a world of difference in the type of service you receive. The first thing I noticed was the way Dmitriy bounded from behind the service counter to greet me. He had just finished waiting on another customer, who was all smiles.

After Dmitriy thanked him and escorted him to the door he gave me a huge smile and said, "How can I be of service to you today?"

I explained that my old vacuum cleaner had finally died and I needed to buy a new one. He asked me what type I had in the past and wanted to know if I had been happy with it. When I told him, he exclaimed, "That's a very good brand and model but unfortunately it's not made anymore. Here's one that I think you'll like because it's of the same high quality."

He let me try it out along with a few others and answered all my questions. It was obvious he had a great deal of knowledge about the pros and cons of each make and model. When I hesitated about buying the vacuum he recommended, he said, "Take it home and try it. Some people think it's a little too heavy and bulky. If you don't like it, we'll find one you do like."

He was so pleasant and so clearly enjoyed what he does that I lingered a bit to chat. He threw in free vacuum cleaner bags and a couple of extra belts for me. Then, he carried the vacuum to the car.

I took it home and tried it. As it turned out, I did find it to be too heavy and bulky for me to push. I called him the next day and he said, "Either you can bring it back or I'll pick it up and drop off another one for you to try." I agreed to bring it back in so I could look at other models.

When I walked in, I was greeted with the same warmth and enthusiasm as he dashed out to my car to carry in the vacuum. He showed me another model that he was sure I'd love but I chose a different vacuum. I got it home, tried it and decided it wasn't the right one. Now I was embarrassed.

I called again and said, "I should have bought the other model you recommended."

"No problem!" Dmitriy joyfully replied. "Do you want me to pick it up?"

I couldn't believe how terrific he was. "No. I'm coming right by there. I'll bring it in and get the other one."

My third visit to Mr. Vak was delightful. Dmitriy said, "Well this is a new record. I've never sold three vacuums in three days to the same person before!"

Not only did he not make me feel bad about my inability to make up my mind, Dmitriy had the new vacuum set up and ready to go for me when I arrived. He called later that day to see if I was happy with my new vacuum.

Here are all the things Dmitriy does right:

♦ He greets each customer as if he or she were an old friend.

♦ He actively listens to his customers' questions and concerns.

♦ He goes the extra mile by carrying the vacuum cleaners to and from his customers' cars.

♦ He's flexible and willing to do everything necessary to make his customers happy.

♦ He clearly does his homework and has extensive knowledge about the products he sells and services.

♦ He rewards his customers and makes them feel special by throwing in a few "extras" at no charge.

This type of service is rare these days. It's no wonder that this store is growing and thriving. Here's an example of a business owner whose actions support his slogan, "Active Sales and Service."

LACK OF FOLLOW-UP
TRANSLATES INTO LOST SALES

Waiting too long to follow up on sales leads has cost me thousands of dollars in lost business. This was one of the most painful mistakes I made during the early years of owning a business. When I waited too long to return a phone call or send out a requested proposal, my prospective clients took their business elsewhere.

Over the years, I have noticed an interesting trend with my business. When I have received inquiries about my services through my website or a referral, the faster I responded, the more likely I was to land the contract. While the following percentages are not scientific, they have held true for my business.

- An inquiry that I respond to the same day I receive it will convert into a sale about 80 percent of the time.

- An inquiry that I respond to within one week of receiving it will convert into a sale about 60 percent of the time.

- An inquiry that I wait more than a week before I respond will convert into a sale about 30 percent of the time.

- Those inquiries that I put aside and respond when I find I have some extra time rarely, if ever, convert into sales.

Your customers and prospects are far too busy to give you a second chance. You either want their business or you don't. If you do, you need to prove it to them. Whether you're in sales or customer service, your response time and attention to details can make or break the deal. A customer or prospect should not be the one doing the work in order to give you their business.

For example, I called a company this morning to inquire about a service they offer. The receptionist informed me that the gentleman I was calling was out of the office. She then said the words that were the kiss of death. "You'll have to call back in about 45 minutes when he returns." She did not ask to take a message. When I asked if he had voice mail, she replied, "No. We don't use voice mail in our office."

Needless to say, they lost the sale already. I will not call back because the one interaction gave me a sample of what I could expect if I took my business to that company. I will not waste my time trying to connect with a person from whom I want to purchase products or services. That's their job.

Here are five tips to increase your sales through effective follow-up:

1. **Recognize that even your existing customers are prospects.** The moment one of your existing customers inquires about making an additional purchase of your products or services, he or she becomes a prospect. Even though an individual is already doing business with you, this may be the moment to increase their level of commitment. Those customers need to be treated like gold.

2. **Call back the same day.**
   When a prospect emails or leaves you a phone message inquiring about a service or product, always return the call on the same day you received it, no matter where you are. I return phone calls from airports, in taxis, between meetings and even during breaks in my seminars. It only takes a moment to return a call. If you know that you won't be able to have a lengthy conversation, explain that you are on a tight time frame but you wanted to call back right away. Then, ask your callers if you may have their permission to call them later that day or tomorrow. This puts them in the driver's seat, because they are directing you as to the time that will work best for them.

3. **If you receive an inquiry via email, send a message back to that individual the same day.**
   Then, pick up the phone to let them know you have replied to their email message and invite them to call if they have questions or need more information. A phone call creates a much stronger connection to callers and demonstrates your commitment to following up on communications.

4. **If you return a call and you get prospective customers' voice mail, leave a message** and ask them to return your call to let you know the best time to reach them the following day. If they tell you they are available at 2:00 p.m. the next day, try to call them precisely at 2:00. They will make a mental note of the fact that you listened to their needs and responded. Even if it turns out they were not there to take your call, they noticed that you kept your promise.

5. **If your prospect requests a proposal for your services, be realistic in your promised date.**
Deliver the proposal exactly on the date promised or a day earlier if possible. Never, ever miss a proposal deadline. If an emergency arises and you know you can't make the deadline, call your prospect well in advance of the due date and request an extension.

The bottom line is this: The way you follow up or fail to follow up with prospective customers will influence the way they perceive your work ethic. No one wants to do business with an individual who cannot be counted on to keep his or her promises.

DO YOUR CUSTOMERS VIEW YOU AS TRUSTWORTHY?

Because I attend so many events, I have the good fortune of meeting and chatting with a wide variety of interesting people. Sometimes these conversations lead to friendships. Other times, they lead to frustration. The frustration occurs when I discover that someone hasn't been honest about his or her intentions.

For example, I met a woman at a conference a couple of years ago. We chatted over lunch and learned we had a lot in common. We both had children late in life. We shared an enthusiasm for outdoor adventure sports and even our husbands had similar careers at that time. When the conference was drawing to a close, she tracked me down and suggested that we meet for lunch some time. I enthusiastically agreed because I had genuinely enjoyed getting to know her and thought it may be the start of new friendship.

True to her word, she called me a couple of weeks later and we scheduled lunch. When I arrived, we greeted each other like old friends and chatted for awhile. So you can imagine my surprise and dismay when she began asking questions about my financial status and retirement plans. You guessed it: She's a financial planner. Suddenly she pulled out this black presentation folder that contained a financial planning guide and sales materials for a variety of investment products. As it turned out, the whole meeting had been a ploy to try to sell me financial services. Had I known, I never would have met with her. I already work with a fantastic financial planner and I wasn't in the market for a new one.

Because I didn't wish to be rude, I graciously ended the lunch and told her I needed to get back to work. She placed the folder in my hands and told me she'd call me soon. She didn't even offer to pay for lunch. It took awhile for the shock to wear off, but when it did, it was replaced with anger. As I drove back to my office, my blood began to boil. I felt betrayed by her dishonesty. I was furious that my time had been wasted and I was angry with myself for being so gullible. The first thing I did when I got back to my office was to throw her presentation folder into the trash basket.

Honesty is a powerful sales strategy that is probably more important today than ever before. If you have integrity, you save your customer time. Time is more precious than money to most people. If your customers cannot trust your every intention, why on earth would they want to do business with you?

Whether you are in sales or customer service, a key question to ask is this: Do your customers view you as trustworthy?" Integrity is not only a question of good morals. Integrity is good business.

Customers want to do business with individuals and companies they can trust. Trust is earned. It cannot be built with one transaction, but it most certainly can be shattered in one transaction. Here are some guidelines for building trust with your customers:

- ♦ **Never lie to a customer about anything.**
  Misleading a customer or leaving out important information is the same as lying. Complete honesty is a must, even if that honesty leads to a customer's decision to stop doing business with you.

◆ **Do what you say you're going to do.**
If you promise anything to a customer, deliver what you've promised. It may be as simple as the promise of a follow-up phone call. Your customers pay attention to the little details. If you're not honest about the small things, they won't trust you to be honest about major transactions.

◆ **Give credit where it's due.**
If a customer compliments you for great service but you know that it was really a co-worker or another department that got the job done, let the customer know.

◆ **Do not criticize your competitors or co-workers.**
When a customer hears you bad-mouthing the competition or a co-worker, your credibility diminishes. Criticizing others is often viewed as a symptom of weak self-confidence. Your customers want assurance that you are confident about the quality of the products or services you offer.

◆ **Be honest about your limitations.**
Expose your weaknesses right up front with your customers. If there are limitations to your product or service, let them know. For example, when I sell my sales training seminars, I don't guarantee that a company's sales will increase by 20%. Instead, I guarantee that I will teach the skills that can signifi-cantly increase sales if members of the sales team implement them correctly.

◆ **Give realistic timetables.**
Nothing is more frustrating to a customer than not receiving a product when they expected it. Don't promise a shipping date that cannot be met. Don't promise that someone from another department will be right with them, and then the customer sits on hold for five minutes. Let your customer know exactly what to expect.

INVITE YOUR CUSTOMERS TO SING YOUR PRAISES

A good customer testimonial is worth its weight in gold. The most effective way to convert prospects into first-time buyers is through testimonials from your satisfied customers.

There are two types of testimonials: unsolicited and solicited. Unsolicited testimonials land on your doorstep without you asking for them. Your customers take the initiative to compliment your products or service and give you permission to quote them.

Solicited testimonials are the comments you invite your customers to give. There are many ways to collect sincere customer testimonials. When you ask for their opinions it not only provides you with great quotes, it also helps you to see the business from their point of view.

Call your customers to thank them for doing business with you. Ask these questions:

- "How are we doing?"
- "How was your last experience with us?"
- "What do you like best about our company, or products, or service?"
- Encourage employees to ask for customer feedback every time they interact with customers. Don't just ask, "How was everything?" Get creative and ask: "Did we do anything to exceed your expectations today?"
- "Our goal was to surprise and delight you with our service. Did we achieve that goal?"
- "What would you tell your friends about what it's like to do business with us?"

Invite your customers to post
their comments on your website.

The folks at Holiday World & Splashin' Safari, a theme and water park in Santa Claus, Indiana, try to take customer service to the extreme. They offer free parking, soft drinks and sunscreen. They have won the title "Friendliest Park on the Planet" for eight consecutive years from the readers of *Amusement Today* magazine. Last year, the park started a "What Our Guests Are Saying" blog a year ago, as a way to get feedback from their customers. They've been flooded with wonderful testimonials.

Get permission to quote your customers and
list their names and credentials.

Customer testimonials are a powerful marketing tool. Be sure to request permission to quote your customers. In order for a testimonial to be truly valuable, it must be believable. Testimonials that include the customer's name, title, company and other information add validity and build customer trust.

Accept the fact that you'll also receive negative
feedback along with positive testimonials.

The more frequently you ask your customers how they feel, the more likely you are to receive some mixed reviews. No problem. A negative comment from a customer can be turned into a positive testimonial if you respond to his or her complaint and make changes to prevent the problem from recurring

YOUR CUSTOMERS ARE YOUR SALES TEAM

Most companies have a budget and a marketing plan but do not devote enough resources to ensuring the highest standards of customer service. Offering the best products in the world will not build customer loyalty. If your customers aren't happy with the service they receive, they won't purchase from you, they won't come back and they'll tell others to stop doing business with you. However, if you have a reasonable product and your customers are delighted with the service, they will keep returning to do business with you. Plus, they will tell others about your products and company.

Word-of-mouth is a powerful marketing tool. Customers who spread good news about your company, products and services are the best sales reps you can have. They are not employees and there is "nothing in it for them" to sell your products and services. So they're perceived as having higher credibility than a paid sales rep.

The majority of the sales process has already been completed when a prospective customer recommended by another customer calls your company. It's much easier to close the sale because trust has been established based solely on the recommendation of their friend or colleague.

So how do you turn your customers into sales reps for your company? It's easy. Simply do the unexpected. Look for ways to surprise and delight each customer who does business with you.

Here are six ways to exceed customer expectations:

1. Test your automated phone system to be sure it is easy for your customers to navigate and always offer them an option to talk to a live person.

2. Don't end any call until you have asked the customer, "Is there anything else I can do for you today?"

3. Thank your customers every time they compliment you or your company.

4. Ask new customers how they learned about your company and, if possible, send a hand-written "thank you" note to the person who referred them.

5. Reward customers for their referrals that turn into business. Send a small gift to the customer who is singing your praises or referring new customers. Base the size of the gift upon the amount of revenue their business and referral generates. I've sent my clients fruit baskets, books, Starbucks® gift cards, flowers and chocolates.

6. Follow up with your customers when they least expect it. Call five customers each week just to say "thank you" and tell them how much you appreciate their business. You can also use these conversations to ask for suggestions on how you or the company can do a better job of providing service. Be sure to listen carefully. They'll give you great ideas.

AFTERWORD

CUSTOMER LOYALTY *IS* AN INSIDE JOB

Whether you work for yourself or for a Fortune-500 company, a nonprofit organization, or as a community volunteer, building customer loyalty needs be a top priority. This book has provided stories, tips and a number of self-assessment tools to help you better understand the vital nature of respecting and supporting your customers—the people who depend on you to communicate with integrity. Your attitude, demeanor and commitment are keys to providing exceptional customer service!

When you focus on building customer loyalty, your co-workers and customers will recognize you as a true professional who genuinely cares about quality.

No, it's not always easy—but it is certainly rewarding and fulfilling—emotionally and financially!

I wish you great success in building customer loyalty from the inside out! Loyalty begins with you.

Debra J. Schmidt
Loyalty Leader®

ABOUT THE AUTHOR

Debra J. Schmidt is an author, consultant, trainer and professional speaker. As the owner of *Loyalty Leader®* Inc., Debra has provided training, consulting and keynote addresses for Fortune 500 companies, small businesses, professional organizations and trade associations worldwide. She has developed customer service standards and delivered training for companies such as Northwestern Mutual, Miller Brewing Company, Wells Fargo, Roundy's, American Family Insurance, Kohler Co, Lucent Technologies and the Green Bay Packers.

Ms. Schmidt has a master's degree in journalism and over 28 years of customer service, business management and sales experience in a wide range of industries. Debra was nominated for an Emmy award in 1991 and has won six national marketing awards. In addition to her monthly television appearances on Fox News in Milwaukee, Wisconsin, Debra is a featured guest on radio shows throughout the United States. Her articles have appeared in hundreds of magazines and on-line publications.

Debra is past president of the National Speakers Association-Wisconsin.

Debra is the author of: *The Extra Mile* and *101 Ways to Build Customer Loyalty*. She is also a featured author in the following books: *How You Can Increase Your Sales in Any Economy* and *Chicken Soup for the Christian Woman's Soul*.

For information about Debra J. Schmidt's speaking, training, and consulting services or to subscribe to her FREE email newsletter filled with tips on how to grow YOUR business, visit: www.LoyaltyLeader.com